Contents

D0511588

RIBA Outline Plan of Work 1998

The Work Stages into which the process of designing building projects and administering building contracts may be divided. *(Some variations to the Work Stages apply for design and build procurement.)*

FEASIBILITY

A   Appraisal

Identification of client's requirements and of possible constraints on development. Preparation of studies to enable the client to decide whether to proceed and to select the probable procurement method.

B   Strategic Briefing

Preparation of Strategic Brief by or on behalf of the client confirming key requirements and constraints.
Identification of procedures, organisational structure and range of consultants and others to be engaged for the project.

PRE-CONSTRUCTION PERIOD

C   Outline Proposals

Commence development of Strategic Brief into full Project Brief.
Preparation of Outline Proposals and estimate of cost.
Review of procurement route.

D   Detailed Proposals

Complete development of the Project Brief.
Preparation of Detailed Proposals.
Application for full Development Control approval.

E   Final Proposals

Preparation of Final Proposals for the project sufficient for co-ordination of all components and elements of the project.

F   Production Information

F1 Preparation of production information in sufficient detail to enable a tender or tenders to be obtained.
   Application for statutory approvals.
F2 Preparation of further production information required under the building contract.

G   Tender Documentation

Preparation and collation of tender documentation in sufficient detail to enable a tender or tenders to be obtained for the construction of the project.

H   Tender Action

Identification and evaluation of potential contractors and/or specialists for the construction of the project.
Obtaining and appraising tenders and submission of recommendations to the client.

CONSTRUCTION PERIOD

J   Mobilisation

Letting the building contract, appointing the contractor.
Issuing of production information to the contractor.
Arranging site hand-over to the contractor.

K   Construction to Practical Completion

Administration of the building contract up to and including practical completion.
Provision to the contractor of further Information as and when reasonably required.

L   After Practical Completion

Administration of the building contract after practical completion.
Making final inspections and settling the final account.

Introduction

The RIBA Outline Plan of Work has become recognised throughout the construction industry and is widely used in a variety of ways, both to assist in the management of projects and as a basis for office procedures.

It was updated and approved by RIBA Council in 1998 and provides the framework for the activities in this detailed plan.

This edition of the detailed *Plan of Work* is a substantial reworking of the original document, first published in 1964, to reflect changes in practice, in legislation and the recommendations of the Co-ordinated Production Information Committee, and to include variants for design and build procurement. Reference has also been made to the Latham report *Constructing the Team,* the Construction Industry Board's Working Group papers particularly *Constructing Success, Briefing the Team* and *Partnering in the Team* and to *Rethinking Construction* by the Government sponsored Construction Task Force under Sir John Egan.

Activity schedules

This edition includes activity schedules for a 'fully designed building project' (Part 2) and variants for the procurement of 'Employer's Requirements' (Part 3) and of 'Contractor's Proposals' (Part 4). Guidance on the tasks that may be necessary in the Feasibility Work Stages A and B is given in Part 1.

'The Plan of Work for a fully designed building project' (Part 2) sets out in a logical fashion the activities of the architect normally necessary for the successful completion of Work Stages C-L in the *RIBA Outline Plan of Work.* The related activities of other contributors to the design process are also shown.

The activity schedules cover outputs (tasks) and process but the lists are not intended to be exhaustive or imperative.

The Services Supplement to the Standard Form of Agreement for the Appointment of an Architect (SFA/99) or Conditions of Engagement for the Appointment of an Architect (CE/99) set out typical design and management services to be performed by the architect. Generally, the activities listed for the architect in this Plan of Work correspond to and amplify those typical services and the related procedures.

The variants of the Plan for design and build procurement (Parts 3 and 4) relate to the architect's services where amendments Design and Build: Employer's Requirements (DB1/99) and/or Design and Build: Contractor's Proposals (DB2/99) are incorporated.

The need for adaptation or expansion of the model to suit the requirements of each project and for each practice, and for careful monitoring of consequences when the logical sequence of events is disturbed or delayed, cannot be over-emphasised.

The relevant activity schedules (Parts 2, 3 or 4) might be used as a basis for a project specific model or, if appropriate, to complement the Services Supplement in architects' agreements SFA/99 or CE/99. They might also be used in conjunction with or substituted for the schedule of services in the agreements of other consultants in order to achieve co-ordination of the activities of the consultant team.

Where the client organisation has established its own procedures, the Plan of Work may also provide a useful basis for checking that those procedures cover all that has to be decided.

The Plan of Work may not be relevant to the architect's activities under the Small Works form of appointment (SW/99), which is for use with projects 'of a straightforward nature where, for instance, the cost of construction works is not expected to exceed £150,000 …'. Nevertheless delivery of such projects will benefit from an execution plan covering procedures and activity sequences which might be derived from the Plan of Work.

Understanding the Model Plan

This section includes some notes on the assumptions made in developing the model plan and on some of the matters, that must be considered in order to confirm or modify application of the Plan of Work, together with a note on the role of the client, and on the briefing process.

Assumptions

In developing the models, certain assumptions are made:
- The appointment of a consultant team, comprising architect, quantity surveyor, structural engineer, building services engineer and planning supervisor.
- The architect is appointed under an RIBA form of appointment (SFA/99 or CE/99 with amendment DB1/99 and/or DB2/99 where appropriate), and the planning supervisor is appointed under RIBA form Appointment as Planning Supervisor (PS/99) with responsibility for preparing the pre-tender Health and Safety Plan.
- The architect performs the roles of lead consultant and contract administrator (or employer's agent), as well as those of designer and design leader.
- The consultants are to perform services to deliver a complete cost planned design.
  NB: Some activities will therefore be additional to those that are described as 'normal' or 'basic' services in the relevant forms of appointment published by the Association of Consulting Engineers or the Royal Institution of Chartered Surveyors.
- All consultants are required to co-operate with and provide information needed by others.

Considerations
Client
The client function may be briefly described as the

Introduction

definition of objectives and provision of information about the project and the site, making decisions and performing the client's obligations under the professional services and building contracts.

Briefing
The brief will normally be developed in three phases. In the first phase, the client establishes the need for the project objectives, perhaps by way of a business case.

In the second phase, which is most effective if carried out after completion of feasibility studies and/or option appraisals, the Strategic Brief is developed, by or for the client, from that initial statement to provide sufficient information for the consultants to commence the design process.

In the third phase the Project Brief is developed from the Strategic Brief in parallel with the design process during Work Stages C and D. The purpose is to identify or confirm the detailed requirements for such matters as operational use, quality, environment, budget, programme and procurement. The Project Brief will define all design requirements and for some building types, eg laboratories, health care buildings, etc it may be appropriate to prepare individual room data sheets.

The client and all members of the consultant team should contribute to the process of evaluation, testing and development. Responsibility for approving and publishing the developed brief lies with the client, but the architect or another consultant may be commissioned to carry out the assembly and editing of the final document.

Project management
At the inception of the project the lead consultant should ascertain how the client wishes to deal with various project management matters that are not shown in the Plan of Work, as they are inherently functions of the client (or of a project manager if appointed), for instance:
- defining the client's requirements, identifying constraints;
- developing and maintaining a project strategy;
- the appointment of appropriate professional skills;
- creating a management structure and good communications environment in which all parties can perform effectively;
- developing project procedures, including identifying relevant existing procedures of the client, administrative actions such as contributions to and frequency of progress reports, validation of certificates, invoices, etc;
- developing and managing change control procedures;
- monitoring performance and activity;
- monitoring the programme in respect of decisions and approvals; and so on.

Some guidance on Work Stage Procedures is given on page 8.

Team management
The team management function is shown under two headings in each Plan of Work – 'Architect as Lead Consultant' in the pre-construction period and 'Architect as Lead Consultant/Contract Administrator (or Employer's Agent)' when the tender Stage is reached.

The lead consultant's function may be briefly described as direction, co-ordination, integration and monitoring of the activities of the consultant team; making or obtaining decisions for cost and programme control; communication between client and consultants; reporting to the client.

Co-ordination may include establishing protocols for electronic data interchange (EDI), where required by the client or agreed by the consultants.

Design leadership
Design leadership is another function (separate from team management) provided by the architect, which includes:
- directing the design process;
- co-ordinating the design in relation to the Health and Safety Plan;
- co-ordinating the design related aspects of the Plan of Work;
- establishing the form and content of design outputs, their interfaces and the verification procedure;
- communicating with the client on significant design issues.

Consultants' outputs
In establishing the nature of the outputs of each consultant the architect as design leader should take into account the procurement method and the information required for the tender pricing document. For a fully designed project, the building contract and the tender documents may be based on:
- full bills of quantities; or
- drawings and specification only; or
- schedules of work/rates.

Other factors affecting the integrity of the consultants' outputs will be the extent to which:
- performance, rather than prescriptive, specification is used; and/or
- provisional sums or measurements are included.

It is also important to identify the lead responsibilities for the design of particular aspects of the project, eg drainage above and below ground, for which more than one of the consultants may be competent.

Introduction

Specialist designers

For a fully designed building project some parcels of work may be designed by specialist designers appointed by the client under the direction of one of the consultants.

Where competitive tenders are to be invited for construction of the Specialist Works based on a detailed design and the design services required are similar to those performed by other consultants, the appointment of a specialist as consultant, eg an acoustic engineer, might be appropriate.

Alternatively, the design can be procured from a specialist contractor/sub-contractor, who will also construct the Specialist Works. Where installation or shop drawings of the Specialist Works will be required at an early stage in the construction process, it may be appropriate to appoint the (potential) sub-contractor as the Specialist Designer, perhaps in conjunction with a two-stage tendering process, during the pre-construction period.

In the latter case it will be possible to co-ordinate and integrate the design of the Specialist Works with other design information available at the time of the main contract tender and at the start of construction. This will help to minimise the need for variations arising from integration of the design of the Specialist Works and the risk of consequential delay or disruption during the construction period.

Where design of the Specialist Works is to be carried out in the pre-construction period the design services of the Specialist Designer may be obtained:

1. by execution of an appropriate warranty agreement between client (Employer) and Specialist Designer (Sub-Contractor); or
2. under a separate design agreement, akin to a consultant's agreement.

As complications would arise if the Specialist Designer were preparing design information under a design agreement after appointment as a sub-contractor, the agreement should be compatible with the form of sub-contract.

Cost advice

Cost advice and related professional services can be provided by:
- the quantity surveyor for all elements in the project; or
- the relevant consultant engineer who may provide the cost information and services for the engineering elements. The quantity surveyor then has the responsibility for cost advice for all other elements and for co-ordination of the engineer's cost advice into the overall cost plan.

Site visits

In JCT standard forms of contract the contractor is wholly responsible for carrying out and completing the works. The Plan of Work assumes that a consultant will visit the site:
- for, or in connection with, the administration of the building contract; and
- to monitor that the construction of the consultant's design is generally in accordance with the contract.

If the client additionally requires site inspectors to be employed to supplement the contractor's own inspections and/or for recording day-to-day information about matters affecting the progress of the works they should be appointed under separate agreements. The Plan of Work does not include the activities of such inspectors.

Feedback

The Plan of Work does not include the activities for feedback or post-project evaluation, which are usually provided as additional services if required by the client. Feedback may be required, particularly under partnership agreements:
- as a basis for review of individual performance and rewards; or
- to facilitate improvement in standards and efficiency by practitioners industry wide; or
- as an additional service required by the client for application to other projects.

For maximum benefit the objectives of the exercise should be established at or before the end of Stage C. Typically the evaluation will draw on:
- project benchmarks – the measurable elements of the project from the Strategic Brief, through the progressive changes to the out-turn performance on the basis of regular progress reports and particular objectives relating to the client's business; and
- national benchmarking statistics for construction related issues.

However, architects and other building professionals also need to evaluate their performance in achieving the goals they set for their own businesses. The formal examination of each commission will provide useful data for future commissions on performance, resource usage, and profitability.

Subjective analysis of client satisfaction and of effort and outputs to obtain the commission will also provide vital information for marketing. The discipline of periodic and Work Stage reports (see page 8) can be beneficial to performance and taken in conjunction with staff time sheets and financial records can reduce the time spent on the evaluation process.

Work Stage Procedures

Effective management of the often complex design process requires the adoption of appropriate procedures from the outset. Some guidance on this aspect is given below.

Work Stages

Each Work Stage has the objective of launching the next. The cycle of work in each Stage is:

- stating the objective and assimilation of relevant facts;
- assessment and provision of resources required;
- establishing appropriate procedures;
- planning the work and setting timetables;
- carrying out work; making proposals; and
- making decisions; setting out objectives for the next Stage.

Programmes

Project Programme

At the commencement of the pre-construction period the lead consultant in consultation with the client and the consultant team should develop a project programme from the timetable – the period of time the client wishes to allow for completion of the consultants' services. The project programme will show, *inter alia*, the period for each Work Stage and any critical dates, eg for client occupation/operational use, for submissions, approvals, appointment of contractors, specialists, etc.

Where Stages are fragmented to provide for design or tender of different elements or two Stages are to run concurrently or to overlap this may affect the duration of various activities, but does not otherwise affect the logic of the Plan of Work. Overlapping Stages can be programmed separately to facilitate monitoring of activities in each Stage.

The project programme should be reviewed at the commencement of each Work Stage in consultation with all the parties contributing to that Work Stage.

SFA/99 indicates the Stage by which consultations and submissions for statutory (and other) submissions should be completed. The Plan of Work indicates the earliest and, perhaps, preferred timing of the process. The appropriate time should be indicated in the project programme.

Work Stage programmes

At the commencement of each Work Stage the lead consultant or contract administrator/employer's agent, in consultation with the client and the consultant team should review and develop the project programme in the light of progress achieved and prepare a Work Stage programme.

This Work Stage programme should co-ordinate:

- the timing of activities to be performed during that Work Stage; and
- information to be provided by the client and team members including any work outstanding from the previous Work Stage.

Each team member should review the resources required to maintain the programmed progress.

The effect of unforeseen developments on the Work Stage programme will need to be monitored, eg:

- a change to the brief, the design or the building contract period;
- delay in granting or requirements of planning or building control approvals.

Any interim adjustment affecting the project programme should be agreed with the client.

Progress and Work Stage reports

The lead consultant or contract administrator/employer's agent, in consultation with the consultant team, should prepare and submit to the client periodic progress reports.

A Work Stage report should be prepared at the end of each Stage setting out the co-ordinated proposals for realising the project in accordance with the brief to the level of detail appropriate to that Work Stage and seeking approval to commence the next Work Stage.

In large or complex projects it may be appropriate to report progress on a more frequent and regular basis – perhaps at monthly intervals.

Such reports might identify actual or potential changes to the project, Work Stage or building contract programmes, to the latest approved construction cost, including the effect of any instructions issued, or to the brief and/or the approved design. They should also identify any instructions required and give suggestions for any corrective action required.

The Plan of Work shows that each team member also provides reports to the lead consultant or contract administrator/employer's agent for incorporation into their reports to the client. At the end of the Work Stage these reports should also indicate any work outstanding.

After assessment of Work Stage reports the client should give any necessary instructions and/or authorise commencement of the next Work Stage.

Construction period procedures

At the commencement of the construction Work Stages, the contract administrator/employer's agent in consultation with the client, the consultant team and where appropriate the contractor will establish procedures for and relating to the administration of the building contract, including matters such as:

- reports, site meetings and inspections;

Work Stage Procedures

- commissioning and testing of building services installations;
- managing change control procedures, including authorisation of variations and delegated financial limits;
- requirements for further information for construction;
- commenting on and issue of contractor's design information, if any;
- establishment of procedures for compliance with Construction (Design and Management) (CDM) Regulations 1994;
- payment procedures, issue of certificates, notices and instructions.

Maintaining control

A significant contribution to making the process efficient and cost-effective can be achieved if client and designers agree to freeze:
- the developed Project Brief at the end of the Detailed Proposals (Stage D); and
- the design (or content of the Employer's Requirements) at the end of the Final Proposals (Stage E).

Success can be assumed if all concerned take the required actions at the correct times. However, nothing prevents action being taken or decisions being made earlier than shown, but if action or decisions are taken too early, subsequent events may prove the work to have been abortive.

Conversely, actions completed after the programmed dates may have a disruptive effect on the work of other contributors and on the achievement of the project's targets.

It is inevitable that, in practice, circumstances will cause a number of departures from the logical course indicated in the model plans, some of these factors will be unforeseen and others will arise from second thoughts.

It cannot be over-emphasised, however, that the greater the number of unplanned departures the greater the risk of loss of control and abortive work. A Plan of Work is essentially a tool for planning and co-ordinating activities that must be tailored to suit the particular circumstance and used in conjunction with the procedures adopted for the project. The Plan of Work alone should not become a 'strait-jacket' imposing inappropriate discipline.

Part 1:
Feasibility Stages

The purpose of Work Stage A – Appraisal – is to clarify the project objectives and determine the best way of proceeding. If studies confirm that a building project is appropriate the key targets are set down in Work Stage B – Strategic Briefing – in sufficient detail to allow the subsequent design and construction phases to be carried out efficiently and cost-effectively.

These notes will not apply to a contractor client preparing to make Contractor's Proposals to the employer (client). Some typical activities by the contractor client and the consultants at the initial stage are given in Part 4.

NB The nature of the process means that there are no 'normal services' which cover Stages A and B. All services must be instructed on the basis of need.

Pre-Stage A: Establishing need
It is fairly obvious that to get to the starting point for any project the client has to identify its objective and what costs are affordable.

A company executive, whether responsible for buying and maintaining the transport fleet, for IT services or for property matters, faced with a problem to be solved or requiring an improvement in facilities or contemplating business expansion, would prepare an outline business case demonstrating the options, the benefits gained, probable capital cost and profitability, and the chance of success before initiating any procurement.

All clients should be advised to carry out this sort of investigation to ascertain the nature of the 'need' and the consequences of satisfying it. It is at this stage that it should become apparent if construction works are necessary to achieve the objectives.

Clients may find that some preliminary advice from an architect or other building professional will help with these matters and, if construction appears to be necessary, in setting the parameters for the 'Appraisal' Stage.

Clients should also be advised to appoint at an early stage a representative, sometimes called the 'project sponsor', who will be the focal point throughout the life of the project for establishing the project parameters, for enquiries and decision making and for liaison with consultants and others providing services. Depending on the scale of the project, the representative may need support from an in-house team including users.

Work Stage A: Appraisal
'Identification of client's requirements and of possible constraints on development. Preparation of studies to enable the client to decide whether to proceed and to select the probable procurement method.'

The tasks to be undertaken at this Stage will vary from project to project, but the first step is to determine the level of detail the client requires to make the decision to proceed.

An activity schedule for the range of matters that may need to be considered by the architect and other building professionals at this time is shown on pages 12 and 13.

It is perhaps inevitable that the client's objectives will include 'aspirations'. One of the outcomes of the Appraisal Stage will be to refine or confirm these elements as 'deliverables'.

Options appraisal
In some cases the Appraisal Stage is simply to confirm that the objectives are reasonably attainable and affordable, this may or may not require preliminary design work. In other cases the process may have to be more rigorous where factors, such as those listed below, are fundamental to the success of the project.
- Functional performance.
- Quality, architectural profile, corporate image.
- Programme for operational use.
- Available finance.
- Value for money.

Where this is the case the number of options (which can multiply exponentially unless a firm grip is maintained on reality) to be investigated and the basis for their appraisal must be carefully considered.

An option appraisal is a comparative analysis of available alternatives in which matters relevant to the client's objectives are scored on a common basis. Where some factors are ranked higher than others the comparative scores for such factors can be weighted accordingly. During the appraisal process some options may be discarded and/or others added.

For projects where work is to be carried out on an existing site, the number of options will be limited and largely concerned with alternative design and/or cost solutions. On the other hand, if a building is required in a new location the options might include existing properties for sale or lease as well as sites for new construction. On such a project, as well as the investigation of the physical environment, appraisals may have to cover the availability of labour, accessibility, transport links etc, and the financial consequences of each option. On occasion it may be appropriate to include a 'do nothing' option as a basis for confirming the parameters.

To complete the appraisal, a report comparing the available and practical solutions, observations on suitable procurement options and the range of professional skills required, is prepared as a basis for the client's decisions on the next steps.

Preferred solution
It may be that the client will require further development of the preferred solution as an aid to the preparation of the Strategic Brief in the next Work Stage, particularly for complex building projects.

Work Stage A:
Appraisal

CLIENT	ARCHITECT AS **LEAD CONSULTANT**	ARCHITECT AS **DESIGNER** AND **DESIGN LEADER**
Determine objectives and scope of the appraisal Authorise commencement of Work Stage Provide initial statement of requirements	Commence Work Stage Receive initial statement of requirements	Commence Work Stage Receive initial statement of requirements
Identify available site(s)	Receive site information, visit site(s), appraise constraints	Receive site information, visit site(s), appraise constraints
Consider evaluation, agree options, the basis for appraisal, programme and instruct LC	Evaluate initial brief Advise on available options, a basis for appraisal and programme	Evaluate initial brief Identify options for consideration Advise on programme
FOR EACH SITE		
Identify site ownership/property condition, boundaries, easements, covenants etc and any operational hazards Consider request for surveys etc and instruct LC	Initiate site appraisal[*] Request approval for necessary site surveys, investigations etc and instruct CT *Certify payments arising*	Contribute to site appraisal[*] Identify surveys required *Carry out or arrange and supervise agreed surveys.* *Validate any payments arising*
FOR EACH OPTION		
Consider design studies with design leader	Co-ordinate preparation of design studies	Prepare design studies Consider comments and amend design as necessary Consult local or other statutory authorities as necessary
	Co-ordinate cost studies	Provide information for initial capital and revenue (facilities management) cost studies Assess risks[**]
OPTIONS APPRAISAL		
Contribute to appraisal of options Advise decision about value management or cost benefit studies Review Report; identify preferred solution	Co-ordinate appraisal of options Consider with client the need for value management or cost benefit studies and if instructed co-ordinate studies Prepare and submit Appraisal Stage Report	Contribute to appraisal of options If instructed, contribute to value management or cost benefit studies.
PREFERRED SOLUTION		
Instruct development of preferred solution as aid to preparation of Strategic Brief Advise decision about Outline Development Control submission	Co-ordinate development of preferred solution Request client instruction for Outline Development Control approval, and direct CT	Develop preferred solution Consider need for Outline Development Control approval and *if instructed make submission*
Prepare outline business case	Co-ordinate provision by CT of information for preparation of outline business case	Provide information for outline business case

Notes

Services in Stages A and B must be instructed on the basis of need

[*] appraisal of physical data, Development Control and environmental impact issues

[**] Risks include uncertainty in programme, cost, external approvals etc.

CT Consultant Team
LC Lead Consultant

QUANTITY SURVEYOR	STRUCTURAL ENGINEER	SERVICES ENGINEER	PLANNING SUPERVISOR
Commence Work Stage	Commence Work Stage	Commence Work Stage	Commence Work Stage
Receive initial statement of requirements	Receive initial statement of requirements	Receive initial statement of requirements	Receive initial statement of requirements
Receive site information, visit site(s), appraise constraints	Receive site information, visit site(s), appraise constraints	Receive site information, visit site(s), appraise constraints	Receive Site information, visit site, appraise constraints
Evaluate initial brief Assist with identification of options Advise on programme	Evaluate initial brief Assist with identification of options Advise on programme	Evaluate initial brief Assist with identification of options Advise on programme	Evaluate initial brief Assist with identification of options Advise on programme
Advise on cost aspects for site appraisal[*]	Advise on structural aspects for site appraisal[*]	Advise on services availability and strategies for site appraisal[*]	
	Identify surveys required Carry out or arrange and supervise agreed surveys Validate any payments arising	Identify surveys required Carry out or arrange and supervise agreed surveys Validate any payments arising	Advise on need for surveys in connection with health and safety risks
Advise on cost aspect of design studies	Advise on structural aspects of design studies	Advise on services aspects of design studies	Advise on safety aspects of design studies
	Consult local or other statutory authorities as necessary	Consult local or other statutory authorities as necessary	
Prepare initial capital cost studies of option Assess risks[**]	Provide information for initial capital and revenue (facilities management) cost studies Assess risks[**]	Provide information for initial capital and revenue (facilities management) cost studies Assess risks[**]	
Contribute to appraisal of options If instructed, contribute to value management or cost benefit studies	Contribute to appraisal of options If instructed, contribute to value management or cost benefit studies	Contribute to appraisal of options If instructed, contribute to value management or cost benefit studies	Contribute to appraisal of options
Prepare cost report on preferred solution as developed Provide information to support submission for Outline Development Control approval	Contribute to development of preferred solution Provide information to support submission for Outline Development Control approval	Contribute to development of preferred solution Provide information to support submission for Outline Development Control approval	Contribute to development of preferred solution
Provide information for outline business case	Provide information for outline business case	Provide information for outline business case	

Work Stage B:
Strategic Briefing

'Preparation of Strategic Brief by or on behalf of the client confirming key requirements and constraints. Identification of procedures, organisational structure and range of consultants and others to be engaged for the project.'

The Strategic Brief is the client's specification of requirements for the project from which the outline design will be developed. It should be in sufficient detail for the consultants to carry out their duties, as it is likely to form the contractual basis for their appointment.

It is the responsibility of the client to prepare the brief. This might be undertaken by the client appointed project sponsor or project manager or the architect as lead consultant. The consultants providing services in the Appraisal Stage might also contribute to its preparation.

The table below indicates the range of subjects that may need definition and possible contributors.

	CLIENT	ARCHITECT as LEAD CONSULTANT	ARCHITECT as DESIGNER	QUANTITY SURVEYOR	STRUCTURAL ENGINEER	SERVICES ENGINEER	PLANNING SUPERVISOR
Preparation of Strategic Brief	✓						
User requirements	✓		✓				
Schedules of accommodation	✓		✓				
Site information	✓		✓		✓	✓	
Design and material quality	✓		✓		✓	✓	
Facilities management	✓		✓		✓	✓	
Environmental services	✓		✓			✓	
Sustainable development policy	✓		✓		✓	✓	
Whole life costing	✓			✓			
Timetable of critical events	✓	✓					
Target cost/cashflow constraints	✓			✓			
Procedures, time and cost controls	✓	✓		✓			
Professional appointments	✓	✓					
Partnering	✓	✓					
Construction procurement	✓	✓		✓			
Value management policy	✓	✓		✓			

Part 2
Plan of Work for a fully designed building project

This co-ordinated Plan of Work for a consultant team operation relates to the traditional fully designed procurement route and is compatible with procurement of the construction of that design under:
• JCT Standard Form of Building Contract 1998 Edition; or
• JCT Intermediate Form of Building Contract 1998 Edition; or
• JCT Standard Form of Prime Cost Contract 1998 Edition; or
• JCT Standard Form of Management Contract 1998 Edition.

The co-ordinated Plan of Work provides guidance for each Work Stage and for each role on the sequence of activities to be performed to achieve completion of each Work Stage. However, it is not intended to provide an exhaustive or imperative list of activities.

It should be noted that the Plan of Work shows that the Brief should be frozen at the end of Stage D, and that the design should be frozen at the end of Stage E.

Activities identified in the co-ordinated Plan of Work in *italics* identify activities that if performed by the consultant may generate the entitlement to a fee adjustment.

The following abbreviations are used in the Co-ordinated Plan of Work:

CA   Lead consultant and contract administrator. The consultant given the authority and responsibility by the client to co-ordinate the services of the other consultants in the construction period and for administration of the building contract;

CT   Consultant team;

H&S   Health and Safety (CDM Regulations);

LC   Lead consultant. The consultant given the authority and responsibility by the client to co-ordinate the services of the other consultants in the pre-construction period;

PS   Planning supervisor. The person engaged to fulfil the statutory requirement.

Work Stage C:
Outline Proposals – Fully Designed Building Project

CLIENT	ARCHITECT AS LEAD CONSULTANT	ARCHITECT AS DESIGNER AND DESIGN LEADER
Authorise commencement of Work Stage Provide Strategic Brief Identify any client's agent or another client; make declaration to HSE	Commence Work Stage Receive Strategic Brief Review with client the impact of CDM Regulations	Commence Work Stage Receive initial statement of requirements
Provide information about site/property condition and any operational hazards (CDM Reg 11)	Receive site information, visit site, appraise constraints[1]	Receive site information, visit site, appraise constraints[1]
Consider evaluation, and sustainable development, provide additional information required and instruct LC	Evaluate Strategic Brief[2] and consider findings with client	Evaluate initial brief[2] Advise on sustainable development
Consider request for surveys etc and instruct LC	Request approval for necessary site surveys, investigations etc and instruct CT *Certify payments arising*	Identify surveys required *If instructed carry out or arrange and supervise agreed surveys. Validate any payments arising*
Consult PS as necessary, appoint additional consultants	Identify requirement for additional consultants, request client sanction	Establish design management procedures
Authorise Project Programme Advise on client procedures Implement Work Stage procedures and programme	Prepare Project Programme Establish Work Stage procedures and programme	Advise on Project Programme Implement Work Stage and design management procedures and programme Prepare initial design studies
Consider design studies with design leader		Consider comments on design studies Consider design studies with client
Participate in development of Project Brief Sanction energy targets and fuel policy	Participate in development of Project Brief Request client sanction to energy targets and fuel policy	Participate in development of Project Brief Advise on energy conservation, agree energy targets
		Initiate preliminary consultations with statutory authorities *(or other persons)*
	Review H&S risk assessments with PS	Review H&S risk assessments with PS
		Prepare Outline Proposals[3] and provide information for initial cost studies Advise on procurement options
Review Work Stage report; instruct LC	Prepare and submit Work Stage report and identify any instructions required	Contribute to Work Stage report, identify any instructions required
	Amend Outline Proposals if instructed to change (or comply with) the brief and direct CT	*Amend Outline Proposals if instructed to change (or comply with) the brief*
Advise decision about Outline Development Control submission	Review need for Outline Development Control approval, request client instructions and direct CT	Consider need for Outline Development Control approval *If instructed make submission for Outline Development Control*
	Request authority to proceed to next Work Stage	Obtain authority to proceed to next Work Stage via LC

Notes

[1] Assessment of physical, environmental, functional and regulatory constraints

[2] Consideration of time/cost/risks and environmental issues; identification of additional information required

[3] In accordance with the Strategic Brief and the developing Project Brief

If post-project evaluation is required the objectives and other arrangements should be established before the end of this stage.

QUANTITY SURVEYOR	STRUCTURAL ENGINEER	SERVICES ENGINEER	PLANNING SUPERVISOR
Commence Work Stage Receive Strategic Brief	Commence Work Stage Receive Strategic Brief	Commence Work Stage Receive Strategic Brief	Commence Work Stage Receive Strategic Brief
Receive site information, visit site, appraise constraints[1]	Receive site information, visit site, appraise constraints[1]	Receive site information, visit site, appraise constraints[1]	Receive Site information, visit site, appraise constraints[1] Open H&S File for the project
Evaluate Strategic Brief Assess economic constraints	Evaluate Strategic Brief[2] Advise on sustainable development	Evaluate Strategic Brief[2] Advise on sustainable development	
	Identify surveys required *If instructed carry out or arrange and supervise agreed surveys Validate any payments arising*	Identify surveys required *If instructed carry out or arrange and supervise agreed surveys Validate any payments arising*	Advise on need for surveys in connection with health and safety risks *If requested advise client about additional consultants*
Advise on Project Programme Implement Work Stage and design management procedures and programme	Advise on Project Programme Implement Work Stage and design management procedures and programme	Advise on Project Programme Implement Work Stage and design management procedures and programme	Advise on Project Programme. Implement Work Stage procedures and programme
	Advise on structural aspects of design studies	Advise on services aspects of design studies	Advise on safety aspects of design studies
Participate in development of Project Brief Advise on cost effect of design and energy options	Participate in development of Project Brief	Participate in development of Project Brief Advise on energy conservation, fuel policy, agree energy targets	
	Initiate preliminary consultations with statutory authorities *(or others)*	Initiate preliminary consultations with statutory authorities *(or others)*	Establish format for pre-tender H&S Plan to be included in tender documents
Review H&S risk assessments with PS	Review H&S risk assessments with PS	Review H&S risk assessments with PS	Review risk assessments with CT. Start to prepare pre-tender H&S Plan
Prepare initial cost plan, including cash flow projection Advise on procurement options	Prepare Outline Proposals[3] and provide information for initial cost studies Advise on procurement options	Prepare Outline Proposals[3] and provide information for initial cost studies Advise on procurement options	Review procurement method in relation to H&S strategy
Contribute to Work Stage report, identify any instructions required	Contribute to Work Stage report, identify any instructions required	Contribute to Work Stage report, identify any instructions required	Contribute to Work Stage report, identify any instructions required
Amend cost plan, including estimate and cash flow, if instructed to change (or comply with) the brief	*Amend Outline Proposals if instructed to change (or comply with) the brief*	*Amend Outline Proposals if instructed to change (or comply with) the brief*	*Advise on H&S aspects of any proposed amendments to Outline Proposals*
If instructed provide information to support Outline Development Control submission	*If instructed provide information to support Outline Development Control submission*	*If instructed provide information to support Outline Development Control submission*	
Obtain authority to proceed to next Work Stage via LC	Obtain authority to proceed to next Work Stage via LC	Obtain authority to proceed to next Work Stage via LC	Obtain authority to proceed to next Work Stage via LC

Work Stage D:

Detailed Proposals – Fully Designed Building Project

CLIENT	ARCHITECT AS LEAD CONSULTANT	ARCHITECT AS DESIGNER AND DESIGN LEADER
Authorise commencement of Work Stage	Commence Work Stage	Commence Work Stage
Implement Work Stage procedures and programme	Implement Work Stage procedures and programme	Implement Work Stage procedures and programme
	Evaluate Outline Proposals to establish compliance with developing brief	Evaluate Outline Proposals, complete and agree user studies to establish compliance with developing brief
Sanction LC report as basis for Detailed Proposals and instruct any changes to developing Brief	Co-ordinate results of CT studies, prepare interim report and request client sanction to continue	Receive design/cost input from CT and develop detailed design solution
Participate in completion of Project Brief	Participate in completion of Project Brief	Participate in completion of Project Brief
Consult PS as necessary, appoint additional consultants, sanction use of specialist designers and instruct LC	Identify requirement for additional consultants and/or design by specialists, request client sanction *Instruct preparation and obtaining of tenders for specialist work*	Identify requirement for additional consultants and/or design by specialists
Instruct LC on equipment tenders Provide details of fixed furniture and equipment to be provided in the building contract	Identify requirement for equipment selection tenders, obtain client sanction *Instruct preparation and obtaining of tenders for equipment*	Prepare Detailed Proposals and outline specification Provide information for elemental cost plan
		Consult and negotiate as necessary to establish compliance in principle with statutory *(and other)* requirements
	Review design co-ordination with PS and CT	Review design co-ordination and development with PS; carry out risk assessments required Provide information to PS for draft pre-tender H&S Plan
Sign off Project Brief	Sign off Project Brief	Sign off Project Brief
PROJECT BRIEF NOW FROZEN		Consolidate Detailed Proposals[4]
	Review procurement advice	
		Update procurement advice
Review Work Stage report, consider risks and any changes required and instruct LC	Prepare and submit Work Stage report and identify any instructions required	Contribute to Work Stage report, identify any instructions required
Authorise detailed Development Control submission	Request client authority for Development Control submission and direct CT	Provide information to support detailed Development Control submission When instructed make submission
	Amend Detailed Proposals if instructed to change (or comply with) the brief and direct CT	*Amend Detailed Proposals if instructed to change (or comply with) the brief*
	Request authority to proceed to next Work Stage	Obtain authority to proceed to next Work Stage via LC

Notes

[4] To include means of escape, fire
     compartments, services space
     requirements, preliminary room
     layouts (if required)

QUANTITY SURVEYOR	STRUCTURAL ENGINEER	SERVICES ENGINEER	PLANNING SUPERVISOR
Commence Work Stage	Commence Work Stage	Commence Work Stage	Commence Work Stage
Implement Work Stage procedures and programme	Implement Work Stage procedures and programme	Implement Work Stage procedures and programme	Implement Work Stage procedures and programme
Evaluate Outline Proposals, complete any necessary cost studies to establish compliance with brief	Evaluate Outline Proposals, complete studies to establish compliance with brief	Evaluate Outline Proposals, complete studies to establish compliance with brief	Evaluate Outline Proposals to establish compliance with any H&S policy decisions in brief
Prepare elemental cost plan	Develop Outline Proposals to identify design constraints etc	Prepare schematic design (based on Outline Proposal)	
Participate in completion of Project Brief	Participate in completion of Project Brief	Participate in completion of Project Brief	Participate in completion of Project Brief
	Identify requirement for additional consultants and/or design by specialists	Identify requirement for additional consultants and/or design by specialists	*Advise client about additional consultants or designers, if requested*
Continuously update cost plan, advise on critical elements	Prepare Detailed Proposals and outline specification Provide information for elemental cost plan	Prepare Detailed Proposals and outline specification Provide information for elemental cost plan	
Advise on cost effects of compliance with statutory *(and other)* requirements	Consult and negotiate as necessary to establish compliance in principle with statutory *(and other)* requirements	Consult and negotiate as necessary to establish compliance in principle with statutory *(and other)* requirements	
Review design co-ordination and development with PS; carry out risk assessments required Provide information to PS for draft pre-tender H&S Plan	Review design co-ordination and development with PS; carry out risk assessments required Provide information to PS for draft pre-tender H&S Plan	Review design co-ordination and development with PS; carry out risk assessments required Provide information to PS for draft pre-tender H&S Plan	Review design co-ordination and development with CT Identify additional risk assessments required Publish draft pre-tender H&S Plan, add relevant information to H&S File
Sign off Project Brief	Sign off Project Brief	Sign off Project Brief	Sign off Project Brief
Prepare firm cost plan and cashflow projection	Update Detailed Proposals[4]	Update Detailed Proposals[4] Negotiate provision of incoming services	Review procurement method in relation to H&S strategy
Review procurement advice	Update procurement advice	Update procurement advice	
Contribute to Work Stage report, identify any instructions required	Contribute to Work Stage report, identify any instructions required	Contribute to Work Stage report, identify any instructions required	Contribute to Work Stage report, identify any instructions required
Provide information to support detailed Development Control submission	Provide information to support detailed Development Control submission	Provide information to support detailed Development Control submission	
Amend cost plan including estimate and cash flow, if instructed to change (or comply with) the brief	*Amend Detailed Proposals if instructed to change (or comply with) the brief*	*Amend Detailed Proposals if instructed to change (or comply with) the brief*	*Advise on H&S aspects of any proposed amendments to Detailed Proposals*
Obtain authority to proceed to next Work Stage via LC	Obtain authority to proceed to next Work Stage via LC	Obtain authority to proceed to next Work Stage via LC	Obtain authority to proceed to next Work Stage via LC

Work Stage E:

Final Proposals – Fully Designed Building Project

CLIENT	ARCHITECT AS LEAD CONSULTANT	ARCHITECT AS DESIGNER AND DESIGN LEADER
Authorise commencement of Work Stage Implement Work Stage procedures and programme	Commence Work Stage Implement Work Stage procedures and programme	Commence Work Stage Implement Work Stage procedures and programme
Sanction final layouts	Request sanction for final layouts	Complete final layouts Receive and incorporate design information from CT Consult statutory authorities *(and others)* on developed design proposals as necessary Agree positions for services terminals, ceiling layouts and major builders' work for services installations
	Make or request decisions necessary to maintain cost control	Provide information for cost checks
		Complete Final Proposals
	Review design co-ordination and development, including design by specialist(s) with PS and CT	Review design co-ordination and development with PS; carry out risk assessments required Provide information to PS for H&S Plan
	Review procurement method and contingency plans	Review design and cost plan Review procurement method and contingency plans
Review Work Stage report, consider risks and any changes required. Instruct LC and PS as necessary	Prepare and submit Work Stage report and identify any instructions required	Contribute to Work Stage report, identify any instructions required
Authorise statutory and other submissions	Arrange programme and obtain client sanction for preparation of and submissions for statutory *(and other)* approvals	Provide information for and make (or support) submissions for statutory *(and other)* approvals
	Amend Final Proposals if instructed to change (or comply with) the brief and direct CT	*Amend Final Proposals if instructed to change (or comply with) the brief*
	Request authority to proceed to next Work Stage	Obtain authority to proceed to next Work Stage via LC

DESIGN (FINAL PROPOSALS) NOW FROZEN

QUANTITY SURVEYOR	STRUCTURAL ENGINEER	SERVICES ENGINEER	PLANNING SUPERVISOR
Commence Work Stage	Commence Work Stage	Commence Work Stage	Commence Work Stage
Implement Work Stage procedures and programme	Implement Work Stage procedures and programme	Implement Work Stage procedures and programme	Implement Work Stage procedures and programme
	Complete sizing of all structural elements Consult statutory authorities *(and others)* on developed design proposals as necessary Provide for integration of services Provide for major builders' work for services installations	Complete final layouts and sizing Consult statutory authorities *(and others)* on developed design proposals as necessary Arrange adequate provision for services integration Agree positions for services terminals, ceiling layouts and major builders' work for services installations	
Continuously check cost of design against cost plan and advise LC	Provide information for cost checks	Provide information for cost checks	
	Complete Final Proposals	Complete Final Proposals	
Review design co-ordination and development with PS; carry out risk assessments required Provide information to PS for H&S Plan	Review design co-ordination and development with PS; carry out risk assessments required Provide information to PS for H&S Plan	Review design co-ordination and development with PS; carry out risk assessments required Provide information to PS for H&S Plan	Review design co-ordination policy with LC and CT Identify additional risk assessments required; update draft H&S Plan, add relevant information to H&S File
Prepare updated cost plan and cashflow projection Review procurement method and contingency plans	Review design and cost plan Review procurement method and contingency plans	Review design and cost plan Review procurement method and contingency plans	Review procurement method in relation to H&S strategy
Contribute to Work Stage report, identify any instructions required	Contribute to Work Stage report, identify any instructions required	Contribute to Work Stage report, identify any instructions required	
Provide information to support statutory *(and other)* submissions	Provide information for and make (or support) submissions for statutory *(and other)* approvals	Provide information for and make (or support) submissions for statutory *(and other)* approvals	
Amend cost plan, including estimate and cash flow if instructed to change (or comply with) the brief	*Amend Final Proposals if instructed to change (or comply with) the brief*	*Amend Final Proposals if instructed to change (or comply with) the brief*	*Advise on H&S aspects of any proposed amendments to the Final Proposals*
Obtain authority to proceed to next Work Stage via LC	Obtain authority to proceed to next Work Stage via LC	Obtain authority to proceed to next Work Stage via LC	Obtain authority to proceed to next Work Stage via LC

Work Stage F:

Production Information – Fully Designed Building Project

CLIENT	ARCHITECT AS **LEAD CONSULTANT**	ARCHITECT AS **DESIGNER** AND **DESIGN LEADER**
Authorise commencement of Work Stage	Commence Work Stage	Commence Work Stage
Implement Work Stage procedures and programme	Implement Work Stage procedures and programme	Implement Work Stage procedures and programme
	F1: Review design co-ordination and development, including design by specialists, with PS and CT	F1: Prepare[5] co-ordinated production information to include: location drawings assembly drawings component drawings schedules : specification
	F2: Identify and agree programme for completion of any outstanding production information	F2: Identify and agree programme for completion of any outstanding production information
	Make or request decisions necessary to maintain cost control	Provide information for cost checks
Review Work Stage report, consider risks and any changes required and instruct LC	Co-ordinate completion of all statutory *(and other)* submissions	Complete all statutory *(and other)* submissions.
	Prepare and submit Work Stage report and identify any instructions required	Contribute to Work Stage report, identify any instructions required
	Amend production information if instructed to change (or comply with) the brief and direct CT	*Amend Production Information if instructed to change (or comply with) the brief*
	Request authority to proceed to next Work Stage	Obtain authority to proceed to next Work Stage via LC
	F2: Request permission to instruct completion of production information in accordance with agreed programme	F2: Complete outstanding production information in accordance with agreed programme when instructed

Notes

Production information may be prepared in two sub-Stages – see Work Stage definition

[5] Includes receiving and integrating information from CT and specialists

[6] BSRIA definitions TN 8/94

ga = general arrangement

QUANTITY SURVEYOR	STRUCTURAL ENGINEER	SERVICES ENGINEER	PLANNING SUPERVISOR
Commence Work Stage	Commence Work Stage	Commence Work Stage	Commence Work Stage
Implement Work Stage procedures and programme	Implement Work Stage procedures and programme	Implement Work Stage procedures and programme	Implement Work Stage procedures and programme
	F1: Prepare[5] co-ordinated production information to include: location drawings (ga) assembly drawings component drawings schedules : specification calculations F2: Identify and agree programme for completion of any outstanding production information	F1: Prepare [5] [6] co-ordinated production information to include: schematic drawings detailed design drawings co-ordination drawings builders work and fixings schedules : specification design criteria : calculations F2: Identify and agree programme for completion of any outstanding production information	Review design co-ordination procedures with LC and CT Identify further information required for pre-tender H&S File
Continuously check cost of design against cost plan and advise LC	Provide information for cost checks	Provide information for cost checks	
Prepare updated cost plan	Complete all statutory (and other) submissions	Complete all statutory (and other) submissions	Review H&S principles and time allocated for completion of project
Contribute to Work Stage report, identify any instructions required	Contribute to Work Stage report, identify any instructions required	Contribute to Work Stage report, identify any instructions required	Contribute to Work Stage report, identify any instructions required
Amend cost plan, including estimate and cash flow, if instructed to change (or comply with) the brief	Amend production information if instructed to change (or comply with) the brief	Amend production information if instructed to change (or comply with) the brief	Advise on H&S aspects of any proposed amendments
Obtain authority to proceed to next Work Stage via LC	Obtain authority to proceed to next Work Stage via LC	Obtain authority to proceed to next Work Stage via LC	Obtain authority to proceed to next Work Stage via LC
F2: Complete outstanding production information in accordance with agreed programme	F2: Complete outstanding production information in accordance with agreed programme	F2: Complete outstanding production information in accordance with agreed programme	

Work Stage G:
Tender Documentation – Fully Designed Building Project

CLIENT	ARCHITECT AS **LEAD CONSULTANT**	ARCHITECT AS **DESIGNER** AND **DESIGN LEADER**
Authorise commencement of Work Stage	Commence Work Stage	Commence Work Stage
Implement Work Stage procedures and programme	Implement Work Stage procedures and programme	Implement Work Stage procedures and programme
	Co-ordinate activities for preparation of pre-tender H&S Plan	Provide final information for pre-tender H&S Plan Finalise all matters arising from statutory and other submissions
Sanction recommended contract conditions	Receive PS and CT advice on contract conditions Advise recommended contract conditions to client	Advise on contract conditions, to include preliminaries, contingencies access and sequence
	Implement document control for tender and contract Co-ordinate production by CT and specialists of Information Release Schedules if required	Issue production information for preparation of tender pricing document and pre-tender estimate[7] Edit production information as necessary Prepare Information Release Schedules if required
	Review procurement method and contingency plans	Review completed production information, pre-tender estimate and contingency plans
Review Work Stage report, consider risks and any changes required and instruct LC	Prepare and submit Work Stage report and identify any instructions required	Contribute to Work Stage report, identify any instructions required
	If instructed by client amend tender documentation to change (or comply with) the brief and direct CT	*If instructed amend tender documentation to change (or comply with) the brief*
	Request authority to proceed to next Work Stage Request sanction to invite tenders [8]	Obtain authority to proceed to next Work Stage via LC

Notes

[7] Responsibility for preparation of tender pricing documents for nominated or named sub-contractors to be confirmed by LC

[8] Contract administrator must sanction the request. LC pre-construction management functions complete

QUANTITY SURVEYOR	STRUCTURAL ENGINEER	SERVICES ENGINEER	PLANNING SUPERVISOR
Commence Work Stage	Commence Work Stage	Commence Work Stage	Commence Work Stage
Implement Work Stage procedures	Implement Work Stage procedures	Implement Work Stage procedures	Implement Work Stage procedures
Provide final information for pre-tender H&S Plan Receive final H&S Plan for incorporation in tender documents	Provide final information for pre-tender H&S Plan Finalise all matters arising from statutory and other submissions	Provide final information for pre-tender H&S Plan Finalise all matters arising from statutory and other submissions	Finalise and issue pre-tender H&S Plan for incorporation in tender documents
Advise on contract conditions, to include preliminaries, contingencies access and sequence	Advise on contract conditions, to include preliminaries, contingencies access and sequence	Advise on contract conditions, to include preliminaries, contingencies access and sequence	Advise on contract conditions in respect of H&S matters including arrangements for design input by contractors and sub-contractors
Receive data for preparation of tender pricing documents[7] Prepare, check and print tender pricing documents[7] Archive data used for tender pricing document	Issue production information for preparation of tender pricing documents[7] Edit production information as necessary. Prepare Information Release Schedules if required	Issue production information for preparation of tender pricing documents[7] Edit production information as necessary. Prepare Information Release Schedules if required	
Review completed production information. Provide pre-tender estimate and updated cashflow projection	Review completed production information, pre-tender estimate and contingency plans	Review completed production information, pre-tender estimate and contingency plans	
Contribute to Work Stage report, identify any instructions required	Contribute to Work Stage report, identify any instructions required	Contribute to Work Stage report, identify any instructions required	
Amend pre-tender estimate, cash flow projection and tender documentation if instructed to change (or comply with) the brief	*Amend tender documentation if instructed to change (or comply with) the brief*	*Amend tender documentation if instructed to change (or comply with) the brief*	*Advise on H&S aspects of any proposed amendments*
Obtain authority to proceed to next Work Stage via LC	Obtain authority to proceed to next Work Stage via LC	Obtain authority to proceed to next Work Stage via LC	Obtain authority to proceed to next Work Stage via LC

Work Stage H:

Tender Action – Fully Designed Building Project

CLIENT	ARCHITECT AS LEAD CONSULTANT AND CONTRACT ADMINISTRATOR	ARCHITECT AS DESIGNER AND DESIGN LEADER
Authorise commencement of Work Stage Sanction tender invitation	Commence Work Stage	Commence Work Stage
Implement Work Stage procedures and programme	Implement Work Stage procedures and programme	Implement Work Stage procedures and programme
Identify any procedural requirements, eg approved contractors, EC directives	Co-ordinate pre-tender enquiries; place EC or other advertisement	Assist with pre-tender enquiries, EC or other advertisement
	Co-ordinate financial and technical checks, consult with PS, select short list of tenderers	Assist with carrying out checks on potential contractors and sub-contractors and preparation of tender short list
Confirm tenderers to CA	Request client sanction	
	Arrange tender invitation, despatch and return. Agree responsibilities	Provide tender documents
		Receive, collate and despatch tender documents for any sub-contract (as allocated by CA)
	Answer tenderers' queries	Assist CA to answer queries
Receive and open tenders (or agree other arrangements)	Co-ordinate appraisal of tenders	
	Receive PS advice on response to pre-tender H&S Plan submitted by preferred tenderer	
Authorise negotiations with tenderer(s) on request of CA	Co-ordinate any agreed negotiations with tenderer(s) authorised by CA/client	Assist with appraisal of tenders and any negotiations with tenderer(s) authorised by CA/client
Review Tender (Work Stage) report, consider risks and any changes required Instruct CA	Prepare and submit Tender (WS) report, identify any instructions required	Contribute to Tender (WS) report, identify any instructions required
Appoint site inspectors if required	*If instructed arrange for adjustment of tender sum/pricing documents and agreement with contractor-elect*	*If instructed amend production information to meet adjustments in the tender sum*
	Co-ordinate any revisions to Production Information	
	Request authority to proceed to next Work Stage	Obtain authority to proceed to next Work Stage via LC

QUANTITY SURVEYOR	STRUCTURAL ENGINEER	SERVICES ENGINEER	PLANNING SUPERVISOR
Commence Work Stage	Commence Work Stage	Commence Work Stage	Commence Work Stage
Implement Work Stage procedures and programme	Implement Work Stage procedures and programme	Implement Work Stage procedures and programme	Implement Work Stage procedures and programme
Assist with pre-tender enquiries, EC or other advertisement Assist with carrying out checks on potential contractors and sub-contractors and preparation of tender short list	Assist with pre-tender enquiries, EC or other advertisement Assist with carrying out checks on potential contractors and sub-contractors and preparation of tender short list	Assist with pre-tender enquiries, EC or other advertisement Assist with carrying out checks on potential contractors and sub-contractors and preparation of tender short list	Advise client on up to 8 prospective tenderers in respect of H&S matters and attend interviews as necessary *Advise on more than 8 prospective tenderers*
Provide tender documents Receive and collate tender documents for main contract (as allocated by CA) Assist CA to answer queries	Provide tender documents Receive, collate and despatch tender documents for any sub-contract (as allocated by CA) Assist CA to answer queries	Provide tender documents Receive, collate and despatch tender documents for any sub-contract (as allocated by CA) Assist CA to answer queries	Assist CA to answer queries in relation to H&S Plan
Assist with appraisal of tenders and any negotiations with tenderer(s) authorised by CA/client	Assist with appraisal of tenders and any negotiations with tenderer(s) authorised by CA/client	Assist with appraisal of tenders and any negotiations with tenderer(s) authorised by CA/client	Appraise response to pre-tender H&S Plan including any method statements, programme etc submitted by preferred tenderer Advise client and CA about preferred tenderer as principal contractor
Contribute to Tender (WS) report, identify any instructions required	Contribute to Tender (WS) report, identify any instructions required	Contribute to Tender (WS) report, identify any instructions required	
If instructed prepare pricing documents for adjustment of the tender sum and agree with contractor-elect Revise cash flow projection	*If instructed amend production information to meet adjustments in the tender sum*	*If instructed amend production information to meet adjustments in the tender sum*	*Advise on H&S aspects of any proposed amendments to the production information*
Obtain authority to proceed to next Work Stage via LC	Obtain authority to proceed to next Work Stage via LC	Obtain authority to proceed to next Work Stage via LC	Obtain authority to proceed to next Work Stage via LC

Work Stage J:

Mobilisation – Fully Designed Building Project

CONTRACTOR	CLIENT	ARCHITECT AS LEAD CONSULTANT AND CONTRACT ADMINISTRATOR	ARCHITECT AS DESIGNER AND DESIGN LEADER
	Authorise commencement of Work Stage and preparation for acceptance of tender Implement Work Stage procedures and programme	Commence Work Stage Implement Work Stage procedures and programme	Commence Work Stage Implement Work Stage procedures and programme
Develop H&S Plan sufficiently for construction phase to commence and agree with PS	Consider letter of acceptance of tender and appointment of principal contractor (CDM Regs) Instruct CA	When H&S Plan sufficiently developed confirm to client that contractor may be appointed and construction may commence	
Execute contract documents and return to CA for completion by client Receive certified true copy of contract documents	Receive, check and execute contract; send certified true copy of Agreement only to CA	Collate sets of contract documents and despatch to contractor for checking and execution. On return, despatch to client for execution Collate certified true copy of all documents for contractor	Contribute to preparation or assembly of main contract or sub-contract documents
Receive production information		Co-ordinate issue of production information	Provide and issue production information
		Brief site inspectorate	Brief site inspectorate
Agree administrative arrangements with CA Complete nominated or named sub-contracts		Agree administrative arrangements with contractor Nominate or name sub-contractors and suppliers	Implement administrative arrangements Contribute to nomination or naming procedures
		Confirm readiness to proceed to client. Request authority to proceed to next Work Stage	Obtain authority to proceed to next Work Stage via CA

QUANTITY SURVEYOR	STRUCTURAL ENGINEER	SERVICES ENGINEER	PLANNING SUPERVISOR
Commence Work Stage	Commence Work Stage	Commence Work Stage	Commence Work Stage
Implement Work Stage procedures and programme	Implement Work Stage procedures and programme	Implement Work Stage procedures and programme	Implement Work Stage procedures and programme
			Review principal contractor's development of H&S Plan and notify client and CA when H&S Plan has been sufficiently developed for construction phase to commence
Contribute to preparation or assembly of contract documents	Contribute to preparation or assembly of main contract or sub-contract documents	Contribute to preparation or assembly of main contract or sub-contract documents	
			Notify further particulars to HSE
Provide production information and priced tender documents for issue	Provide production information for issue	Provide production information for issue	
Brief site inspectorate	Brief site inspectorate	Brief site inspectorate	
Implement administrative arrangements Contribute to nomination or naming procedures	Implement administrative arrangements Contribute to nomination or naming procedures	Implement administrative arrangements Contribute to nomination or naming procedures	Review design co-ordination procedures in respect of information provided by contractors and specialists with CA and contractor
Obtain authority to proceed to next Work Stage via CA	Obtain authority to proceed to next Work Stage via CA	Obtain authority to proceed to next Work Stage via CA	Obtain authority to proceed to next Work Stage via CA

Work Stage K:

Construction to Practical Completion – Fully Designed Building Project

CONTRACTOR	CLIENT	ARCHITECT AS **LEAD CONSULTANT** AND **CONTRACT ADMINISTRATOR**	ARCHITECT AS **DESIGNER** AND **DESIGN LEADER**
Take possession of site	Authorise commencement of Work Stage and arrange hand-over of site to contractor Implement Work Stage procedures and programme	Commence Work Stage Implement Work Stage procedures and programme	Commence Work Stage Implement Work Stage procedures and programme
Perform the obligations of the contractor under the building contract Obtain design information for comment by CA and designers Contribute to calculation of value interim certificates Continuously assemble data for H&S File	Consider proposed variations exceeding delegated limits Instruct CA, adjusting approved cost if necessary Honour certificates by due date Instruct ascertainment of loss and/or expense if requested	Administer the terms of the contract, eg: • issue information[9] and instructions required[10] requesting PS sanction where necessary *Request approval if delegated limits will be exceeded* • issue interim certificates; notifying nominated or named sub-contractors • consider claims received and give decisions • ascertain loss and/or expense	Provide additional information[9] reasonably required Advise on the need for variations *If instructed provide information for variations* Examine and comment on design information [9] provided by or through contractor, advise CA as necessary Advise on work included in interim certificates *Assist with evaluation of claims*
Prepare regular progress reports Attend CA progress and performance review meetings Conduct meetings as required for proper management of the contract	Consider progress and financial statements. Instruct CA as necessary	Receive CT, contractors and site inspector(s)'s reports Conduct progress and performance review meetings with CT and contractor Attend contractor's meetings as appropriate Prepare and issue monthly reports on progress, out-turn cost and cash flow	Make site visits and report to CA Contribute to progress and performance review meetings Attend contractor's meetings as appropriate
Agree procedures for and carry out commissioning and testing of services	Agree commissioning and testing procedures. Witness M&E tests if desired Appoint/allocate staff to receive training	Agree commissioning and testing procedures for services, including drainage, with contractor and client	
Provide completed information for H&S File and Building Owners Manual as specified		Co-ordinate preparation of Building Owner's Manual with H&S File Co-ordinate inspection of the Works	Receive specified data from contractor, incorporate in Building Owner's Manual Inspect the Works
Confirm that all works are complete Attend hand-over meeting[11] Agree defects reporting procedure	Attend meeting[11] and receive Works for occupation or use Implement defects reporting procedure Arrange insurance	On contractor's confirmation that all works are complete, hold hand-over meeting[11] Agree defects reporting procedure Advise client to insure building	Attend hand-over meeting[11], confirm completion of outstanding items
	Honour interim certificate	Issue certificate(s) of practical completion and interim certificate(s) and updated status report Request authority to proceed to next Work Stage	Obtain authority to proceed to next Work Stage via CA

Notes

[9] Information includes:
• further production information
• Contractor's Statements
• Contractor's Proposals

• installation/shop drawings
• builder's work details
• manufacturer's data
• method statements

[10] Consider need for and cost of variations proposed, obtaining contractor's quotation, where appropriate

[11] Tour the Works; client receives keys from contractor and Building Owner's Manual from CA and H&S File from PS

QUANTITY SURVEYOR	STRUCTURAL ENGINEER	SERVICES ENGINEER	PLANNING SUPERVISOR
Commence Work Stage	Commence Work Stage	Commence Work Stage	Commence Work Stage
Implement Work Stage procedures and programme	Implement Work Stage procedures and programme	Implement Work Stage procedures and programme	Implement Work Stage procedures and programme
Advise on financial effect of contract administration Estimate cost of proposed or issued variations	Provide additional information[9] reasonably required Advise on the need for variations *If instructed provide information for variations* Examine and comment on design information [9] provided by or through contractor, advise CA as necessary	Provide additional information[9] reasonably required Advise on the need for variations *If instructed provide information for variations* Examine and comment on design information [9] provided by or through contractor, advise CA as necessary	Review further information[9] including information from (or through) contractor, ensuring H&S implications have been considered and relevant information provided to contractor *Examine draft design variation instructions to contractor, ensure health and safety implications have been considered and relevant information provided to contractor*
Prepare valuation statements for interim certificates	Advise on work included in interim certificates	Advise on work included in interim certificates	
Assist with evaluation of claims	*Assist with evaluation of claims*	*Assist with evaluation of claims*	
Prepare regular cost reports including out-turn cost and cash flow Contribute to progress and performance review meetings	Make site visits and report to CA Contribute to progress and performance review meetings	Make site visits and report to CA Contribute to progress and performance review meetings	
Attend contractor's meetings as appropriate	Attend contractor's meetings as appropriate	Attend contractor's meetings as appropriate	
		Co-ordinate commissioning and testing procedures for services *Witness tests* Examine and comment on results and records of commissioning Arrange for training of client's personnel (as contract)	
	Receive specified data from contractor, incorporate in Building Owner's Manual	Receive specified data from contractor, incorporate in Building Owner's Manual	Receive, review and collate information from CT and from (or through) contractor and add to H&S File
	Inspect the Works	Inspect the Works	
	Attend hand-over meeting[11], confirm completion of outstanding items	Attend hand-over meeting[11], confirm completion of outstanding items	Attend hand-over meeting[11], deliver completed H&S File to client Advise on secure storage and future use of File
Prepare valuation statements for interim certificates Review and issue updated cost report at completion Obtain authority to proceed to next Work Stage via CA	Obtain authority to proceed to next Work Stage via CA	Obtain authority to proceed to next Work Stage via CA	Advise client that (consultant) Services are complete
Building Owner's Manual may include: • drawings of the building and the main lines of drainage; • drawings of building services installations;	• test results, commissioning records, certificates for building services installations; • information required for operation of the facilities; • general advice on maintenance.	The Manual may be combined with the H&S File	*NB: Drawings of the building as built, maintenance and operational manuals, planned maintenance schedules, etc specially prepared by the consultant may be 'Additional Services'.*

Work Stage L:

After Practical Completion – Fully Designed Building Project

CONTRACTOR	CLIENT	ARCHITECT AS **LEAD CONSULTANT** AND **CONTRACT ADMINISTRATOR**	ARCHITECT AS **DESIGNER** AND **DESIGN LEADER**
	Authorise commencement of Work Stage	Commence Work Stage	Commence Work Stage
	Implement Work Stage procedures and programme	Implement Work Stage procedures and programme	Implement Work Stage procedures and programme
Correct defects in accordance with agreed procedure	Report defects that require immediate attention as they occur	Receive defect reports, determine necessary action and instruct contractor	Advise on necessary action for defects
Collaborate in assembly of data and agree matters for final account and Final Certificate		Review decisions affecting completion date within 12 weeks of practical completion	Advise CA on extensions of time review
	Consider reports	Submit regular reports to client	
	Honour interim certificates	Issue interim certificates as necessary	
Collaborate in pre-final inspections	Collaborate in pre-final inspections	Co-ordinate pre-final inspections, collate and issue schedules of defects including incomplete work	Make pre-final inspections and prepare schedule of defects and incomplete work
Agree programme for execution of any remedial works with client and CA	Agree programme for any remedial work	Liaise with client and contractor to agree programme	
	Appoint PS if necessary	Advise client if planning supervisor should be (re)appointed to prepare H&S Plan for repair of any major defects	
Confirm that all remedial works are complete	Collaborate in final inspection	When contractor confirms work is complete, arrange and make final inspection	Make final inspections and confirm that all works are complete
Receive certificate(s) of making good defects		Issue certificate(s) of making good defects	
Agree final account prior to receipt of Final Certificate			
	Honour Final Certificate	Issue Final Certificate	
		Advise client that (consultant) Services are complete	Advise client that (consultant) Services are complete

QUANTITY SURVEYOR	STRUCTURAL ENGINEER	SERVICES ENGINEER	PLANNING SUPERVISOR
Commence Work Stage	Commence Work Stage	Commence Work Stage	
Implement Work Stage procedures and programme	Implement Work Stage procedures and programme	Implement Work Stage procedures and programme	
Obtain information required to settle final account within time stated in contract	Advise on necessary action for defects	Advise on necessary action for defects	
Update last cost report if predicted out-turn cost changes	Advise CA on extensions of time review	Advise CA on extensions of time review	
Advise on value of interim certificates if appropriate			
	Make pre-final inspections and prepare schedule of defects and incomplete work	Make pre-final inspections and prepare schedule of defects and incomplete work	
	Make final inspections and confirm that all works are complete	Make final inspections and confirm that all works are complete	
Complete final account and agree with contractor Issue final account to CA			
Advise client that (consultant) Services are complete	Advise client that (consultant) Services are complete	Advise client that (consultant) Services are complete	

Part 3

Plan of Work for procurement of Employer's Requirements

This variant of the co-ordinated Plan of Work for consultant team operation relates to the procurement of the Employer's Requirements and is compatible with procurement of the design and construction of those requirements under the *JCT Standard Form of Building Contract With Contractor's Design 1998 Edition*. This Plan of Work, like JCT WCD 98, is suitable for the several options in this procurement family, ie design and build, design and construct, etc.

The Plan of Work provides guidance for each Work Stage and for each role on the sequence of activities to be performed to achieve completion of each Work Stage. However, it is not intended to provide an exhaustive or imperative list of activities.

It will be noted that the Plan provides for the brief to be frozen at the end of Stage D, but if the Employer's Requirements will not include any design the activities to be performed in Stage C will need to be varied and include the complete development of the Project Brief.

Activities identified in the co-ordinated Plan of Work in *italics* identify activities that if performed by the consultant may generate the entitlement to a fee adjustment.

It will be noted that the roles of employer/client and contractor are also particular to the procurement route.

Work Stages for Procurement of Employer's Requirements

The objective of each Work Stage for projects using the design and build procurement route is described overleaf. The Work Stages have the same titles as the *RIBA Outline Plan of Work*, but Stages G, H and J are modified for this procurement method.

The Work Stages relevant to the work of the consultant team will be dependent on the extent to which the client wishes to pre-determine the design and constructional detail for the project.

At one extreme, the client may wish the design to be virtually complete, perhaps including bills of quantities and/or specified sub-contractors for all or some elements, in this case the relevant Pre-Construction Work Stages will be C to H.

At the other extreme, the client may simply wish to give minimal information leaving the selected or tendering contractors to prepare the conceptual and the detailed design, in this case the relevant Pre-Construction Work Stages will be C (excluding design), G and H.

Most projects using this method of procurement will probably fall somewhere between the two extremes. It should be remembered however that the risk to the employer client's targets for time, cost and quality are dependent on the integrity of the information included in the Employer's Requirements.

The following abbreviations are used in the co-ordinated Plan of Work:

CT Consultant team;

EA Employer's agent. The person engaged by the employer client to perform the employer's agent function;

H&S Health and Safety (CDM Regulations);

LC Lead consultant. The consultant given the authority and responsibility by the client to co-ordinate and monitor the activities of the other consultants;

PS Planning supervisor. The person engaged to fulfil the statutory requirement.
Note: This role may be performed by the contractor after acceptance of a tender.

RIBA Outline Plan of Work 1998

For Employer's Requirements

The objective during the Work Stages C to G (or such other Stages as may be agreed for the project) prior to inviting tenders at Stage H is to develop the 'Employer's Requirement' document by way of prescriptive information or by performance specification and in sufficient detail to identify the allocation of risk between the client and the contractor.

FEASIBILITY

A Appraisal
Identification of client's requirements and of possible constraints on development. Preparation of studies to enable the client to decide whether to proceed and to select the probable procurement method.

B Strategic Briefing
Preparation of Strategic Brief by or on behalf of the client confirming key requirements and constraints.
Identification of procedures, organisational structure and range of consultants and others to be engaged for the project.

PRE-CONSTRUCTION PERIOD

C Outline Proposals
Commence development of Strategic Brief into full Project Brief.
Preparation of Outline Proposals and estimate of cost.
Review of procurement route.

D Detailed Proposals
Complete development of the Project Brief.
Preparation of Detailed Proposals.
Application for full Development Control approval.

E Final Proposals
Preparation of Final Proposals for the project sufficient for co-ordination of all components and elements of the project.

F Production Information
F1 Preparation of production information in sufficient detail to enable a tender or tenders to be obtained.
Application for statutory approvals.
F2 Stage F2 not required for Design and Build.

G Tender Documentation
Preparation and collation of tender documentation **(comprising the Employer's Requirements and the tender pricing documents)** in sufficient detail to enable **potential contractor's to prepare and submit a price and Contractor's Proposals** a tender or tenders to be obtained for the construction of the project.

H Tender Action
Identification and evaluation of potential contractors and/or specialists for the construction of the project.
Obtaining and appraising tenders **and Contractor's Proposals** and submission of recommendations to the client.

CONSTRUCTION PERIOD

J Mobilisation
Letting the building contract, appointing the contractor. Issuing of production information to the contractor. Arranging site hand-over to the contractor. **Review of further Contractor's Proposals.**

K Construction to Practical Completion
Administration of the building contract up to and including practical completion.
Provision to the contractor of further Information as and when reasonably required.

L After Practical Completion
Administration of the building contract after practical completion.
Making final inspections and settling the final account.

Employer's Requirements

The Employer's Requirement document is the basis for obtaining tenders and is created during the Pre-Construction Work Stages C to G (or such other Stages as may be agreed for the project) prior to inviting tenders at Stage H.

**Delete as applicable

It might comprise**:

Preliminaries and Contract Conditions

JCT WCD 98 Supplementary Provisions
S2 Submission of drawings
S3 Site Manager
S4 Named sub-contractors
S5 Bills of Quantities
S6 Valuation of change instructions
S7 Direct loss and/or expense

Evaluation, monitoring, and verification
procedures and criteria
Information requirements
Pre-tender Health and Safety Plan

Contextual information

Brief
Client's Health and Safety Policy
Site constraints (covenants etc)
Topographical surveys
Geo-technical report
Existing engineering services and/or main supplies
Planning consent – outline/detailed/reserved matters
Statutory consultation records
Room data sheets

Design intent

(all or part may be by way of performance specification)
1:100 Plans, sections and elevations
1:500 Site layout, including critical setting out data
1:50 room layout plans
Site – extent, external works and access
Landscape design
Fire compartments and escape routes
Engineering services mains and risers
Plant spaces
Drainage – main runs
Enabling works

Specification

Quality – aesthetics and other subjective considerations
Constraints
Materials and workmanship
Technical standards
Building Owners Manual – operation and maintenance
Health and Safety File

Performance standards

for all Work Groups

Schedules

Equipment including sanitary and storage fittings,
user outlets, etc

Commissioning and testing

Work Stage C:

Outline Proposals – Employer's Requirements

EMPLOYER CLIENT	ARCHITECT AS LEAD CONSULTANT	ARCHITECT AS DESIGNER AND DESIGN LEADER
Authorise commencement of Work Stage Provide Strategic Brief	Commence Work Stage Receive Strategic Brief	Commence Work Stage Receive Strategic Brief
Identify any client's agent or another client; declaration to HSE	Review with employer client the impact of CDM Regulations	
Provide information about site/property condition and any operational hazards (CDM Reg 11)	Receive site information, visiting site, appraise constraints[1]	Receive site information, visit site, appraise constraints[1]
Consider evaluation and sustainable development, provide additional information required and instruct LC	Evaluate Strategic Brief[2] and consider findings with employer client	Evaluate Strategic Brief[2] Advise on sustainable development
Consider request for surveys etc and instruct LC	Request approval for necessary site surveys, investigations etc and instruct CT *Certify payments arising*	Identify surveys required *If instructed carry out or arrange and supervise agreed surveys. Validate any payments arising*
Consult PS as necessary, appoint additional consultants	Identify requirement for additional consultants, obtain client sanction	Establish design management procedures
Authorise Project Programme Advise on employer client procedures Implement Work Stage procedures and programme	Prepare Project Programme Establish Work Stage procedures and programme	Advise on Project Programme Implement Work Stage and design management procedures and programme Prepare initial design studies
Consider design studies with design leader		Consider comment on design studies Consider design studies with client
Participate in development of Project Brief Sanction energy targets and fuel policy	Participate in development of Project Brief Request client sanction to energy targets and fuel policy	Participate in development of Project Brief Advise on energy conservation, agree energy targets
		Implement preliminary consultations with statutory authorities *(or other persons)*
	Review H&S risk assessments with PS	Review H&S risk assessments with PS
		Prepare Outline Proposals[3] and provide information for initial cost studies Advise on procurement options
Review Work Stage report; instruct LC	Prepare and submit Work Stage report and identify any instructions required	Contribute to Work Stage report, identify any instructions required
	Amend Outline Proposals if instructed to change (or comply with) the brief and direct CT	*Amend Outline Proposals if instructed to change (or comply with) the brief*
Advise decision about Outline Development Control submission	Review need for Outline Development Control approval, request employer client's instructions. Direct CT	Consider need for Outline Development Control approval *If instructed make submission for Outline Development Control*
	Request authority to proceed to next Work Stage	Obtain authority to proceed to next Work Stage via LC

[1] Assessment of physical environmental, functional and regulatory constraints	[2] Consideration of time/cost/risks and environmental issues; identification of additional information required	[3] In accordance with the Strategic Brief and the developing Project Brief

QUANTITY SURVEYOR	STRUCTURAL ENGINEER	SERVICES ENGINEER	PLANNING SUPERVISOR
Commence Work Stage Receive Strategic Brief	Commence Work Stage Receive Strategic Brief	Commence Work Stage Receive Strategic Brief	Commence Work Stage Receive Strategic Brief Review with employer client the impact of CDM Regulations Notify project to HSE
Receive site information, visit site, appraise constraints[1]	Receive site information, visit site, appraise constraints[1]	Receive site information, visit site, appraise constraints[1]	Receive site information, visit site, appraise constraints[I] Open H&S File for the project
Evaluate Strategic Brief Assessment of economic constraints	Evaluate Strategic Brief[2] Advise on sustainable development	Evaluate Strategic Brief[2] Advise on sustainable development	
	Identify surveys required	Identify surveys required	Advise need for surveys in connection with health and safety risks
	If instructed carry out or arrange and supervise agreed surveys Validate any payments arising	*If instructed carry out or arrange and supervise agreed surveys Validate any payments arising*	
			If requested advise employer client about additional consultants
Advise on Project Programme Implement Work Stage and design management procedures and programme	Advise on Project Programme Implement Work Stage and design management procedures and programme	Advise on Project Programme Implement Work Stage and design management procedures and programme	Advise on Project Programme Implement Work Stage and design management procedures and programme
	Advise on structural aspects of design studies	Advise on services aspects of design studies	Advise on safety aspects of design studies
Participate in development of Project Brief Advise cost effect of design and energy options	Participate in development of Project Brief	Participate in development of Project Brief Advise on energy conservation, fuel policy, agree energy targets	
	Implement preliminary consultations with statutory authorities *(or others)*	Implement preliminary consultations with statutory authorities *(or others)*	Establish format for pre-tender H&S Plan to be included in tender documents
Review H&S risk assessments with PS	Review H&S risk assessments with PS	Review H&S risk assessments with PS	Review risk assessments with CT. Start to prepare pre-tender H&S Plan
Prepare initial cost plan, including cash flow projection[3] Advise on procurement options	Prepare Outline Proposals[3] and provide information for initial cost plan Advise on procurement options	Prepare Outline Proposals[3] and provide information for initial cost plan Advise on procurement options	Review procurement method in relation to H&S strategy
Contribute to Work Stage report, identify any instructions required	Contribute to Work Stage report, identify any instructions required	Contribute to Work Stage report, identify any instructions required	
Amend cost plan, including estimate and cash flow, if instructed to change (or comply with) the brief	*Amend Outline Proposals if instructed to change (or comply with) the brief*	*Amend Outline Proposals if instructed to change (or comply with) the brief*	*Advise H&S aspects of any proposed amendments to Outline Proposals*
If instructed provide information to support Outline Development Control submission	*If instructed provide information to support Outline Development Control submission*	*If instructed provide information to support Outline Development Control submission*	
Obtain authority to proceed to next Work Stage via LC	Obtain authority to proceed to next Work Stage via LC	Obtain authority to proceed to next Work Stage via LC	Obtain authority to proceed to next Work Stage via LC

If post-project evaluation is required the objectives
and other arrangements should be established
before the end of this stage.

Work Stage D:

Detailed Proposals – Employer's Requirements

EMPLOYER CLIENT	ARCHITECT AS LEAD CONSULTANT	ARCHITECT AS DESIGNER AND DESIGN LEADER
Authorise commencement of Work Stage	Commence Work Stage	Commence Work Stage
Implement Work Stage procedures and programme	Implement Work Stage procedures and programme	Implement Work Stage procedures and programme
	Evaluate Outline Proposals to establish compliance with developing brief	Evaluate Outline Proposals, complete and agree user studies to establish compliance with developing brief
Sanction LC report as basis for Detailed Proposals and instruct any changes to brief	Co-ordinate results of CT studies, prepare interim report and request client sanction to continue	Receive design/cost input from CT and develop detailed design solution
Participate in completion of Project Brief	Participate in completion of Project Brief	Participate in completion of Project Brief
Consult PS as necessary, appoint additional consultants, sanction use of specialists and instruct LC	Identify requirement for additional consultants and/or specialists[4A], request employer client sanction	Identify requirement for additional consultants and/or specialists
Provide details of fixed furniture and equipment to be provided in the building contract		Prepare Detailed Proposals and outline specification Provide information for elemental cost plan
		Consult and negotiate as necessary to establish compliance in principle with statutory *(and other)* requirements
	Review design co-ordination with PS and CT	Review design co-ordination and development with PS; carry out risk assessments required Provide information to PS for draft pre-tender H&S Plan
Sign off Project Brief	Sign off Project Brief	Sign off Project Brief
PROJECT BRIEF NOW FROZEN		Consolidate Detailed Proposals[4]
	Review procurement advice	Update procurement advice
Review Work Stage report, consider risks and any changes required and instruct LC	Prepare and submit Work Stage report and identify any instructions required	Contribute to Work Stage report, identify instructions required
Authorise detailed Development Control submission	Request client authority for Development Control submission and direct CT	Provide information to support detailed Development Control submission When instructed make submission
	Amend Detailed Proposals if instructed to change (or comply with) the brief and direct CT	*Amend Detailed Proposals if instructed to change (or comply with) the brief*
	Request authority to proceed to next Work Stage	Obtain authority to proceed to next Work Stage via LC

Notes

[4A] Specialists may be consultants or designers to be named as sub-contractors under clause S4 of JCT WCD 98

[4] To include means of escape, fire compartments, services space requirements, design by specialist(s), preliminary room layouts (if required)

QUANTITY SURVEYOR	STRUCTURAL ENGINEER	SERVICES ENGINEER	PLANNING SUPERVISOR
Commence Work Stage	Commence Work Stage	Commence Work Stage	Commence Work Stage
Implement Work Stage procedures and programme	Implement Work Stage procedures and programme	Implement Work Stage procedures and programme	Implement Work Stage procedures and programme
Evaluate Outline Proposals, complete any necessary cost studies to establish compliance with brief	Evaluate Outline Proposals, complete studies to establish compliance with brief	Evaluate Outline Proposals, complete studies to establish compliance with brief	Evaluate Outline Proposals to establish compliance with any H&S policy decisions in brief
Prepare elemental cost plan	Develop Outline Proposals to identify design constraints etc	Prepare schematic design (based on Outline Proposal)	
Participate in completion of Project Brief	Participate in completion of Project Brief	Participate in completion of Project Brief	Participate in completion of Project Brief
	Identify requirement for additional consultants and/or specialists	Identify requirement for additional consultants and/or specialists	*Advise client about additional consultants or designers, if requested*
Continuously update cost plan, advise on critical elements	Prepare Detailed Proposals and outline specification Provide information for elemental cost plan	Prepare Detailed Proposals and outline specification Provide information for elemental cost plan	
Advise on cost effects of compliance with statutory *(and other)* requirements	Consult and negotiate as necessary to establish compliance in principle with statutory *(and other)* requirements	Consult and negotiate as necessary to establish compliance in principle with statutory *(and other)* requirements	
Review design co-ordination and development with PS; carry out risk assessments required Provide information to PS for draft pre-tender H&S Plan	Review design co-ordination and development with PS; carry out risk assessments required Provide information to PS for draft pre-tender H&S Plan	Review design co-ordination and development with PS; carry out risk assessments required Provide information to PS for draft pre-tender H&S Plan	Review design co-ordination and development with CT. Identify additional risk assessments required Publish draft pre-tender H&S Plan, add relevant information to H&S File
Sign off Project Brief	Sign off Project Brief	Sign off Project Brief	Sign off Project Brief
Prepare firm cost plan and cash flow projection	Update Detailed Proposals[4]	Update Detailed Proposals[4] Negotiate provision of incoming services	
Review procurement advice	Update procurement advice	Update procurement advice	Review procurement method in relation to H&S strategy
Contribute to Work Stage report, identify instructions required	Contribute to Work Stage report, identify instructions required	Contribute to Work Stage report, identify instructions required	Contribute to Work Stage report, identify instructions required
Provide information to support detailed Development Control submission	Provide information to support detailed Development Control submission	Provide information to support detailed Development Control submission	
Amend cost plan, including estimate and cash flow if instructed to change (or comply with) the brief	*Amend Detailed Proposals if instructed to change (or comply with) the brief*	*Amend Detailed Proposals if instructed to change (or comply with) the brief*	*Advise H&S aspects of any proposed amendments to Detailed Proposals*
Obtain authority to proceed to next Work Stage via LC	Obtain authority to proceed to next Work Stage via LC	Obtain authority to proceed to next Work Stage via LC	Obtain authority to proceed to next Work Stage via LC

Work Stage E:

Final Proposals – Employer's Requirements

EMPLOYER CLIENT	ARCHITECT AS LEAD CONSULTANT	ARCHITECT AS DESIGNER AND DESIGN LEADER
Authorise commencement of Work Stage	Commence Work Stage	Commence Work Stage
Implement Work Stage procedures and programme	Implement Work Stage procedures and programme	Implement Work Stage procedures and programme
Sanction final layouts	Request sanction for final layouts	Complete final layouts Receive and incorporate design information from CT Consult statutory authorities *(and others)* on developed design proposals, as necessary Agree positions for services terminals, ceiling layouts and major builders' work for services installations
	Make or request decisions necessary to maintain cost control	Provide information for monthly cost checks
		Complete Final Proposals
	Review design co-ordination and development, including design by specialist(s) with PS and CT	Review design co-ordination and development with PS; carrying out risk assessments required Provide information to PS for H&S Plan
	Review procurement method and contingency plans	Review design, cost plan procurement method and contingency plans
Review Work Stage report, consider risks and any changes required and instruct LC	Prepare and submit Work Stage report and identify any instructions required	Contribute to Work Stage report, identify any instructions required
Authorise statutory and other submissions	Arrange preparation of submissions for statutory *(and other)* approvals Request client sanction	Provide information for and make (or support) submissions for statutory *(and other)* approvals
	Amend Final Proposals if instructed to change (or comply with) the brief and direct CT	*Amend Final Proposals if instructed to change (or comply with) the brief*
	Request authority to proceed to next Work Stage	Obtain authority to proceed to next Work Stage via LC

DESIGN (FINAL PROPOSALS) NOW FROZEN

QUANTITY SURVEYOR	STRUCTURAL ENGINEER	SERVICES ENGINEER	PLANNING SUPERVISOR
Commence Work Stage	Commence Work Stage	Commence Work Stage	Commence Work Stage
Implement Work Stage procedures and programme	Implement Work Stage procedures and programme	Implement Work Stage procedures and programme	Implement Work Stage procedures and programme
	Complete sizing of all structural elements Consult statutory authorities *(and others)* on developed design proposals, as necessary Provide for integration of services Provide for major builders' work for services installations	Complete final layouts and sizing Consult statutory authorities *(and others)* on developed design proposals, as necessary Arrange adequate provision for services integration Agree positions for services terminals, ceiling layouts and major builders' work for services installations	
Continuously check cost of design against cost plan and advise LC	Provide information for cost checks	Provide information for cost checks	
	Complete Final Proposals	Complete Final Proposals	
Review design co-ordination and development with PS; carrying out risk assessments required Provide information to PS for H&S Plan	Review design co-ordination and development with PS; carrying out risk assessments required Provide information to PS for H&S Plan	Review design co-ordination and development with PS; carrying out risk assessments required Provide information to PS for H&S Plan	Review design co-ordination policy with LC and CT Identify additional risk assessments required; update draft H&S Plan, add relevant information to H&S File
Prepare updated cost plan and cash flow projection Review procurement method and contingency plans	Review design and cost plan Review procurement method and contingency plans	Review design and cost plan Review procurement method and contingency plans	Review procurement method in relation to H&S strategy
Contribute to Work Stage report, identify any instructions required	Contribute to Work Stage report, identify any instructions required	Contribute to Work Stage report, identify any instructions required	
Provide information to support statutory *(and other)* submissions	Provide information for and making (or supporting) submissions for statutory *(and other)* approvals	Provide information for and making (or supporting) submissions for statutory *(and other)* approvals	
Amend cost plan, including estimate and cash flow if instructed to change (or comply with) the brief	*Amend Final Proposals if instructed to change (or comply with) the brief*	*Amend Final Proposals if instructed to change (or comply with) the brief*	*Advise on H&S aspects of any proposed amendments to the Final Proposals*
Obtain authority to proceed to next Work Stage via LC	Obtain authority to proceed to next Work Stage via LC	Obtain authority to proceed to next Work Stage via LC	Obtain authority to proceed to next Work Stage via LC

Work Stage F:

Production Information – Employer's Requirements

EMPLOYER CLIENT	ARCHITECT AS LEAD CONSULTANT	ARCHITECT AS DESIGNER AND DESIGN LEADER
Authorise commencement of Work Stage	Commence Work Stage	Commence Work Stage
Implement Work Stage procedures and programme	Implement Work Stage procedures and programme	Implement Work Stage procedures and programme

	Review design co-ordination and development, including design by specialist(s), with PS and CT	Prepare[5] co-ordinated production information to include:
		  location drawings
		  assembly drawings
		  component drawings
		  schedules : specification

	Make or request decisions necessary to maintain cost control	Provide information for continuous cost checks
	Co-ordinate completion of all statutory (and other) submissions	Complete all statutory[7] (and other) submissions.
Review Work Stage report, consider risks and any changes required and instruct LC	Prepare and submit Work Stage report and identify any instructions required	Contribute to Work Stage report, identify any instructions required
	Amend production information if instructed to change (or comply with) the brief and direct CT	*Amend production information if instructed to change (or comply with) the brief*
	Request authority to proceed to next Work Stage	Obtain authority to proceed to next Work Stage via LC

Work Stage G:

Tender Documentation – Employer's Requirements

EMPLOYER CLIENT	ARCHITECT AS LEAD CONSULTANT	ARCHITECT AS DESIGNER AND DESIGN LEADER
Authorise commencement of Work Stage	Commence Work Stage	Commence Work Stage
Implement Work Stage procedures	Implement Work Stage procedures	Implement Work Stage procedures
Sanction recommended contract conditions	Co-ordinate activities for preparation of pre-tender H&S Plan	Provide final information for pre-tender H&S Plan Finalise all matters arising from statutory[6] and other submissions
	Receive PS and CT advice on contract conditions Advise employer client on recommended contract conditions	Advise on contract conditions, to include preliminaries, contingencies access and sequence
	Implement document control procedures for tender and contract	Issue Employer's Requirements for preparation of tender pricing document and pre-tender estimate. Edit as necessary
	Review procurement method and contingency plans	Review completed Employer's Requirements, pre-tender estimate and contingency plans
Review Work Stage report, consider risks and any changes required and instruct LC	Prepare and submit Work Stage report and identify any instructions required	Contribute to Work Stage report, identify any instructions required
	Amend tender documentation if instructed to change (or comply with) the brief and direct CT	*Amend tender documentation if instructed to change (or comply with) the brief*
	Request authority to proceed to next Work Stage Request sanction to invite tenders[8]	Obtain authority to proceed to next Work Stage via LC

Notes

[5] Includes receiving and integrating information from CT and specialists

[6] BSRIA definitions TN 8/94

ga = general agreement

NB: Stage F2 not applicable to design and build procurement

[7] Some statutory submissions may be made by contractor

[8] Employer's Agent must sanction the report. LC pre-construction management functions complete

QUANTITY SURVEYOR	STRUCTURAL ENGINEER	SERVICES ENGINEER	PLANNING SUPERVISOR
Commence Work Stage	Commence Work Stage	Commence Work Stage	Commence Work Stage
Implement Work Stage procedures and programme	Implement Work Stage procedures and programme	Implement Work Stage procedures and programme	Implement Work Stage procedures and programme
	Prepare[5] co-ordinated production information to include: 　location drawings (ga) 　assembly drawings 　component drawings 　schedules : specification 　calculations	Prepare[5] [6] co-ordinated production information to include: 　schematic drawings 　detailed design drawings 　co-ordination drawings 　builders' work and fixings 　schedules : specification 　calculations	Review design co-ordination procedures with LC and CT Identify further information required for pre-tender H&S File
Continuously check cost of design against cost plan and advise LC	Provide information for continuous cost checking	Provide information for continuous cost checking	
Prepare updated cost plan	Complete all statutory[7] (and other) submissions	Complete all statutory[7] (and other) submissions	Review H&S principles and time allocated for completion of project
Contribute to Work Stage report, identify any instructions required	Contribute to Work Stage report, identify any instructions required	Contribute to Work Stage report, identify any instructions required	Contribute to Work Stage report, identify any instructions required
Amend cost plan, including estimate and cash flow, if instructed to change (or comply with) the brief	*Amend Production Information if instructed to change (or comply with) the brief*	*Amend Production Information if instructed to change (or comply with) the brief*	*Advise H&S aspects of any proposed amendments*
Obtain authority to proceed to next Work Stage via LC	Obtain authority to proceed to next Work Stage via LC	Obtain authority to proceed to next Work Stage via LC	Obtain authority to proceed to next Work Stage via LC

QUANTITY SURVEYOR	STRUCTURAL ENGINEER	SERVICES ENGINEER	PLANNING SUPERVISOR
Commence Work Stage	Commence Work Stage	Commence Work Stage	Commence Work Stage
Implement Work Stage procedures	Implement Work Stage procedures	Implement Work Stage procedures	Implement Work Stage procedures
Provide final information for pre-tender H&S Plan Receive final H&S Plan for incorporation in tender documents	Provide final information for pre-tender H&S Plan Finalise all matters arising from statutory[6] and other submissions	Provide final information for pre-tender H&S Plan Finalise all matters arising from statutory[6] and other submissions	Finalise and issue pre-tender H&S Plan for incorporation in tender documents
Advise on contract conditions, to include preliminaries, contingencies access and sequence	Advise on contract conditions, to include preliminaries, contingencies access and sequence	Advise on contract conditions, to include preliminaries, contingencies access and sequence	Advise on contract conditions in respect of H&S matters, including arrangements for design input by contractors and sub-contractors
Receive data for preparation of tender pricing document Prepare, check and print tender pricing document Archive data used for tender pricing document	Issue Employer's Requirements for preparation of tender pricing document. Edit as necessary	Issue Employer's Requirements for preparation of tender pricing document. Edit as necessary	
Provide pre-tender estimate and updated cash flow projection	Review completed Employer's Requirements pre-tender estimate and contingency plans	Review completed Employer's Requirements, pre-tender estimate and contingency plans	
Contribute to Work Stage report, identify any instructions required	Contribute to Work Stage report, identify any instructions required	Contribute to Work Stage report, identify any instructions required	
Amend tender documentation if instructed to change (or comply with) the brief	*Amend tender documentation if instructed to change (or comply with) the brief*	*Amend tender documentation if instructed to change (or comply with) the brief*	*Advise H&S aspects of any proposed amendments*
Obtain authority to proceed to next Work Stage via LC	Obtain authority to proceed to next Work Stage via LC	Obtain authority to proceed to next Work Stage via LC	Obtain authority to proceed to next Work Stage via LC

Work Stage H:

Tender Action – Employer's Requirements

EMPLOYER CLIENT	ARCHITECT AS LEAD CONSULTANT AND EMPLOYER'S AGENT	ARCHITECT AS DESIGNER AND DESIGN LEADER
Authorise commencement of Work Stage Sanction tender invitation Implement Work Stage procedures and programme	Commence Work Stage Implement Work Stage procedures and programme	Commence Work Stage Implement Work Stage procedures and programme
Identify any procedural requirements, eg approved contractors, EC directives Confirm tenderers to EA	Co-ordinate pre-tender enquiries; place EC or other advertisement Co-ordinate financial and technical checks, consult with PS, select short list of tenderers Request client sanction	Assist with pre-tender enquiries, EC or other advertisement Assist with carrying out checks on applicants and preparation of tender short list
	Arrange tender invitation, despatch and return. Agree responsibilities	Provide tender documents
	Answer tenderers' queries	Assist EA to answer queries
Receive and open tenders (or agree other arrangements) Authorise negotiations with tenderer(s) on request of EA	Co-ordinate appraisal of tenders and Contractor's Proposals Co-ordinate any agreed negotiations with tenderer(s) Receive PS advice on H&S Plan submitted by preferred tenderer	Assist with appraisal of tenders and Contractor's Proposals Assist with any negotiations with tenderer(s) authorised by employer client/EA
Review Tender (Work Stage) report, consider risks and any changes required and instruct EA	Prepare and submit Tender (WS) report Identify any instructions required	Contribute to Tender (WS) report, identify any instructions required
Appoint site inspectors if required	*If instructed co-ordinate any revisions to the Employer's Requirements or Contractor's Proposals to meet adjustments in the tender sum or Contract Sum Analysis*	*If instructed amend the Employer's Requirements or Contractor's Proposals to meet adjustments in the tender sum or Contract Sum Analysis*
	Request authority to proceed to next Work Stage	Obtain authority to proceed to next Work Stage via EA

QUANTITY SURVEYOR	STRUCTURAL ENGINEER	SERVICES ENGINEER	PLANNING SUPERVISOR
Commence Work Stage	Commence Work Stage	Commence Work Stage	Commence Work Stage
Implement Work Stage procedures and programme	Implement Work Stage procedures	Implement Work Stage procedures and programme	Implement Work Stage procedures and programme
Assist with pre-tender enquiries, EC or other advertisement Assist with carrying out checks on applicants and preparation of tender short list	Assist with pre-tender enquiries, EC or other advertisement Assist with carrying out checks on applicants and preparation of tender short list	Assist with pre-tender enquiries, EC or other advertisement Assist with carrying out checks on applicants and preparation of tender short list	Advise employer client on up to 8 prospective tenderers in respect of H&S matters and attend interviews as necessary *Advise on more than 8 prospective tenderers*
Provide tender documents Receive and collate tender documents	Provide tender documents	Provide tender documents	
Assist EA to answer queries	Assist EA to answer queries	Assist EA to answer queries	Assist EA to answer queries in relation to H&S Plan
Assist with appraisal of tenders and any negotiations with tenderer(s) authorised by employer client or EA	Assist with appraisal of tenders and Contractor's Proposals Assist with any negotiations with tenderer(s) authorised by employer client/EA	Assist with appraisal of tenders and Contractor's Proposals Assist with any negotiations with tenderer(s) authorised by employer client/EA	Appraise H&S Plan, including any method statements, programme and other relevant documents submitted by preferred tenderer Advise employer client and EA about preferred tenderer as principal contractor
Contribute to Tender (WS) report, identify any instructions	Contribute to Tender (WS) report, identify any instructions	Contribute to Tender (WS) report, identify any instructions	
If instructed prepare pricing documents for adjustment of the tender sum or Contract Sum Analysis and agree with contractor-elect Revise cash flow projection	*If instructed amend the Employer's Requirements or Contractor's Proposals to meet adjustments in the tender sum or Contract Sum Analysis*	*If instructed amend the Employer's Requirements or Contractor's Proposals to meet adjustments in the tender sum or Contract Sum Analysis*	*Advise H&S aspects of any proposed amendments to the Employer's Requirements or Contractor's Proposals*
Obtain authority to proceed to next Work Stage via EA	Obtain authority to proceed to next Work Stage via EA	Obtain authority to proceed to next Work Stage via EA	Obtain authority to proceed to next Work Stage via EA

Work Stage J:

Mobilisation – Employer's Requirements

CONTRACTOR	EMPLOYER CLIENT	ARCHITECT AS LEAD CONSULTANT AND EMPLOYER'S AGENT	ARCHITECT AS DESIGNER AND DESIGN LEADER
	Authorise commencement of Work Stage and preparation for acceptance of tender Implement Work Stage procedures and programme	Commence Work Stage Implement Work Stage procedures and programme	Commence Work Stage Implement Work Stage procedures and programme
Develop H&S Plan sufficiently for construction phase to commence and agree with PS	Consider letter of acceptance of tender and appointment of principal contractor (CDM Regs) and instruct EA	When H&S Plan sufficiently developed confirm to employer client that contractor may be appointed and construction may commence	
Prepare further Contractor's Proposals		Co-ordinate review of further Contractor's Proposals	Review further Contractor's Proposals
Execute contract documents and return to EA for completion by employer client Receive certified true copy of contract documents	Receive, check and execute contract; send certified true copy of Agreement only to EA	Collate sets of contract documents and despatch to contractor for checking and execution. On return, despatch to employer client for execution Collate certified true copy of all documents for contractor	Contribute to preparation or assembly of contract documents
Receive Employer's Requirements		Collate and issue sets of Employer's Requirements	Provide and issue Employer's Requirements
Agree administrative arrangements with EA		Brief site inspectorate	Brief site inspectorate
		Agree with contractor administrative arrangements	Implement administrative arrangements
		Confirm readiness to proceed to client. Request authority to proceed to next Work Stage	Obtain authority to proceed to next Work Stage via EA

QUANTITY SURVEYOR	STRUCTURAL ENGINEER	SERVICES ENGINEER	PLANNING SUPERVISOR
Commence Work Stage	Commence Work Stage	Commence Work Stage	Commence Work Stage
Implement Work Stage procedure and programme	Implement Work Stage procedures and programme	Implement Work Stage procedure and programme	Implement Work Stage procedures and programme
			Review principal contractor's development of H&S Plan and notify employer client and EA when H&S Plan has been sufficiently developed for construction phase to commence
	Review further Contractor's Proposals	Review further Contractor's Proposals	Review further Contractor's Proposals
Contribute to preparation or assembly of contract documents	Contribute to preparation or assembly of contract documents	Contribute to preparation or assembly of contract documents	Notify further particulars to HSE
Provide and issue Employer's Requirements	Provide and issue Employer's Requirements	Provide and issue Employer's Requirements	
	Brief site inspectorate	Brief site inspectorate	Review design co-ordination procedures in respect of information provided by contractors and specialists with EA and contractor
Implement administrative arrangements	Implement administrative arrangements	Implement administrative arrangements	
Obtain authority to proceed to next Work Stage via EA	Obtain authority to proceed to next Work Stage via EA	Obtain authority to proceed to next Work Stage via EA	Obtain authority to proceed to next Work Stage via EA

Work Stage K:

Construction to Practical Completion – Employer's Requirements

CONTRACTOR	EMPLOYER CLIENT	ARCHITECT AS LEAD CONSULTANT AND EMPLOYER'S AGENT	ARCHITECT AS DESIGNER AND DESIGN LEADER
Take possession of site	Authorise commencement of Work Stage and arrange hand-over of site to contractor Implement Work Stage procedures and programme	Commence Work Stage Implement Work Stage procedures and programme	Commence Work Stage Implement Work Stage procedures and programme
Carry out the obligations of the contractor under the building contract Provide further Contractor's Proposals Continuously assemble data for H&S File Calculate and apply for interim payments	Confirm scope of EA's authority Consider proposed change instructions exceeding delegated limits. Instruct EA, increase approved cost if necessary Honour certificate by due date Instruct ascertainment of loss and/or expense if requested	Administer terms of the contract as agent of the employer client, eg: • co-ordinate review of further Contractor's Proposals • issue information and instructions required • consider need for change instructions, requesting contractor's quotation and PS sanction where appropriate • request approval if delegated limits will be exceeded • validate interim payments • consider claims received and give decisions • seek approval to ascertain loss and/or expense where budget may be exceeded	Review further Contractor's Proposals Advise on the need for change instructions *If instructed provide information for change instructions* Advise on work included in interim payments *Assist with evaluation of claims*
Prepare regular progress reports Attend EA progress and performance review meetings Conduct meetings as required for proper management of the contract	Consider progress and financial statements and instruct EA	Receive CT, contractor's and site inspector(s) reports Conduct progress and performance review meetings with CT and contractor Attend contractor's meetings as appropriate Prepare and issue monthly reports on progress, out-turn cost and cash flow	Make site visits and report to EA Contribute to progress and performance review meetings Attend contractor's meetings as appropriate
Agree procedures for and carry out commissioning and testing of services	Agree commissioning and testing procedures. Witness M&E tests if desired Appoint/allocate staff to receive training	Agree commissioning and testing procedures for services, including drainage, with contractor and employer client	
Provide completed information for H&S File and Building Owners Manual as specified		Co-ordinate preparation of Building Owner's Manual with H&S File Co-ordinate inspection of the Works	Receive specified data from contractor, incorporate in Building Owner's Manual Inspect the Works
Confirm that all works are complete Attend hand-over meeting[9] Agree defects reporting procedure	Attend meeting[9] and receive Works for occupation or use Implement defects reporting procedure Arrange insurance	On contractor's confirmation that all works are complete, hold hand-over meeting[9] Agree defects reporting procedure Advise client of need to insure building	Attend meeting[9], confirm completion of outstanding items
	Honour interim certificate	Issue statement(s) of practical completion, validate interim payments and issue updated status report Request authority to proceed to next Work Stage	Obtain authority to proceed to next Work Stage via EA

Notes

[9] Tour the Works; Client receives keys from contractor, Building Owner's Manual from EA and H&S File from PS

QUANTITY SURVEYOR	STRUCTURAL ENGINEER	SERVICES ENGINEER	PLANNING SUPERVISOR
Commence Work Stage	Commence Work Stage	Commence Work Stage	Commence Work Stage
Implement Work Stage procedures and programme	Implement Work Stage procedures and programme	Implement Work Stage procedures and programme	Implement Work Stage procedures and programme
Advise on financial effect of contract administration Estimate/validate cost of proposed or issued change instructions Prepare valuation statements for or validate interim payments	Review further Contractor's Proposals Advise on the need for change instructions *If instructed provide information for change instructions* Advise on work included in interim payments	Review further Contractor's Proposals Advise on the need for change instructions *If instructed provide information for change instructions* Advise on work included in interim payments	Review further Contractor's Proposals, ensuring health and safety implications have been considered *Examine draft design change instructions to contractor, ensuring health and safety implications have been considered and relevant information provided to contractor*
If instructed, assist with evaluation of claims	*Assist with evaluation of claims*	*Assist with evaluation of claims*	
Prepare regular cost reports, including out-turn cost and cash flow Contribute to progress and performance review meetings Attend contractor's meetings as appropriate	Make site visits and report to EA Contribute to progress and performance review meetings Attend contractor's meetings as appropriate	Make site visits and report to EA Contribute to progress and performance review meetings Attend contractor's meetings as appropriate	
		Co-ordinate commissioning and testing procedures for services *Witness acceptance tests* Examine and comment on results and records of commissioning Arrange for training of employer client's personnel (as contract)	
	Receive specified data from contractor, incorporate in Building Owner's Manual Inspect the Works	Receive specified data from contractor, incorporate in Building Owner's Manual Inspect the Works	Receive, review and collate information from CT and contractor and add to H&S File
	Attend meeting[9], confirm completion of outstanding items	Attend meeting[9], confirm completion of outstanding items	Attend meeting[9], deliver completed H&S File to client Advise on secure storage and future use of File
Validate interim payment(s) Review and issue updated cost report at completion Obtain authority to proceed to next Work Stage via EA	Obtain authority to proceed to next Work Stage via EA	Obtain authority to proceed to next Work Stage via EA	Advise client that (consultant) Services are complete

Building Owner's Manual may include:
- 'drawings and information showing or describing the Works as built, and concerning the maintenance operation of the Works, including any installations comprised in the Works, as may be specified…' (clause 5.5 JCT WCD 98); and
- acceptance test results, commissioning records, certificates for building services installations.

The Manual may be combined with the H&S File

Work Stage L:

After Practical Completion – Employer's Requirements

CONTRACTOR	EMPLOYER CLIENT	ARCHITECT AS LEAD CONSULTANT AND EMPLOYER'S AGENT	ARCHITECT AS DESIGNER AND DESIGN LEADER
	Authorise commencement of Work Stage	Commence Work Stage	Commence Work Stage
	Implement Work Stage procedures and programme	Implement Work Stage procedures and programme	Implement Work Stage procedures and programme
Correct defects in accordance with agreed procedure	Report defects which require immediate attention as they occur	Receive defect reports, determine necessary action and instruct contractor	Advise necessary action for defects
Collaborate in assembly of data and agree matters for final account and final statement		Review decisions affecting completion date within 12 weeks of practical completion	Advise EA on extensions of time review
	Consider reports	Submit periodic reports to client	
	Honour interim certificates	Validate interim payments as necessary	
Collaborate in pre-final inspections	Collaborate in pre-final inspections	Co-ordinate pre-final inspections, collate and issue schedules of defects, including incomplete work	Make pre-final inspections and prepare schedule of defects and incomplete work
Agree programme for execution of any remedial works with employer client and EA	Agree programme for any remedial work	Liaise with employer client and contractor to agree programme	
	Appoint PS if necessary	Advise client if Planning Supervisor should be (re)appointed to prepare H&S Plan for repair of any major defects	
Confirm that all remedial works are complete	Collaborate in final inspection	When contractor confirms work is complete, arrange and make final inspection	Make final inspections and confirm that all works are complete
Receive notice(s) of making good defects		Issue notice of making good defects	
Agree final account prior to receipt of final statement			
	Honour final statement	Issue final statement	
		Advise client that (consultant) Services are complete	Advise client that (consultant) Services are complete

QUANTITY SURVEYOR	STRUCTURAL ENGINEER	SERVICES ENGINEER	PLANNING SUPERVISOR
Commence Work Stage	Commence Work Stage	Commence Work Stage	Commence Work Stage
Implement Work Stage procedures and programme	Implement Work Stage procedures and programme	Implement Work Stage procedures and programme	Implement Work Stage procedures and programme
Obtain information required to settle final account within time stated in contract	Advise necessary action for defects	Advise necessary action for defects	
Update last cost report if predicted out-turn cost changes	Advise EA on extensions of time review	Advise EA on extensions of time review	
Validate interim payments as necessary			
	Make pre-final inspections and prepare schedule of defects and incomplete work	Make pre-final inspections and prepare schedule of defects and incomplete work	
	Make final inspections and confirm that all works are complete	Make final inspections and confirm that all works are complete	
Complete final account and agree with contractor Issue final account to EA			
Advise client that (consultant) Services are complete	Advise client that (consultant) Services are complete	Advise client that (consultant) Services are complete	

Part 4

Plan of Work for procurement of Contractor's Proposals

This variant of the co-ordinated Plan of Work for consultant team operation relates to the procurement of the Contractor's Proposals and is compatible with procurement of the design and construction of those proposals under the *JCT Standard Form of Building Contract With Contractor's Design 1998 Edition.* This Plan of Work, like JCT WCD 98, is suitable for the several options in this procurement family, ie design and build, design and construct, etc.

The Plan of Work provides guidance for each Work Stage and for each role on the sequence of activities to be performed to achieve completion of each Work Stage. However, it is not intended to provide an exhaustive or imperative list of activities.

It should be remembered that the risk to the contractor client's targets for time, cost and quality are dependent on the integrity of the information included in the Contractor's Proposals.

Activities identified in the co-ordinated Plan of Work in *italics* identify activities that if performed by the consultant may generate the entitlement to a fee adjustment.

Work Stages for Procurement of Contractor's Requirements

The co-ordinated Plan of Work is based on special Work Stages applicable to the development of contractor's proposals from the 'Employer's Requirements' and the services that may be required by a contractor client.

The objective of each of these special Work Stages, pre-fixed 'CP', is described overleaf. The Work Stages have the same titles as the *RIBA Outline Plan of Work,* but some of the descriptions reflect the particular nature of a contractor client's requirements.

The Work Stages relevant to the work of the consultant team and their timing will be dependent on the extent to which the contractor client or the Employer's Requirements and/or the tender invitation require the design and constructional detail to be developed at tender Stage.

For instance, if the Employer's Requirements give minimal information and require the contractor's proposals only to be developed to the end of Stage D before tender, the order would be Work Stages CP/A, CP/C, CP/D and CP/G and CP/H. After acceptance of the contractor client's tender the Work Stages would be CP/J, CP/E, CP/F, CP/K and CP/L.

It will be noted that although submission of the project for detailed Development Control Approval is indicated at Stage D other statutory or other approvals are deferred until after acceptance of the Contractor's tender at Stage J – Mobilisation.

The following abbreviations are used in the Co-ordinated Plan of Work:

CC   Contractor client. Responsible for the design and construction of the project in accordance with the contractor's obligations under the building contract;

CT   Consultant team. Responsible for the design of the Contractor's Proposals;

EA   Employer's agent. The person engaged by the employer to perform the employer's agent function;

H&S   Health and Safety (CDM Regulations);

LC   Lead consultant. The consultant given authority and responsibility by the contractor client to co-ordinate and monitor the activities of the other consultants;

PS   Planning supervisor. The person engaged to fulfil the statutory requirement.
      Note: This role may be performed by a consultant appointed by the employer or by the contractor client if the building contract so requires.

RIBA Outline Plan of Work 1998

For Contractor's Proposals

The special Work Stages that the process of preparing Contractor's Proposals (completion of design) under a design and build contract may be divided as follows:

FEASIBILITY

CP/A **Appraisal**
Review of Employer's Requirements and of possible constraints on development. Preparation of studies to enable the Contractor client to decide on appropriate design and construction approaches.

CP/B **Strategic Briefing**
Preparation of contractor client's policy statement incorporating the Employer's Requirements. Identification of procedures, organisational structure and range of consultants and others to be engaged for the project.

PRE-CONSTRUCTION PERIOD

CP/C **Outline Proposals**
Preparation of Outline Proposals and estimate of cost.

CP/D **Detailed Proposals**
Preparation of Detailed Proposals. Application for full Development Control approval.

CP/E **Final Proposals**
Preparation of final proposals for the project sufficient for co-ordination of all components and elements of the project.

CP/F **Production Information**
F1 Preparation of production information if required for tender submission.
F2 Preparation of (further) production information required for construction.

CP/G **Tender Documentation**
Preparation and collation of tender submission documentation.

CP/H **Tender Action**
Contractor client's tender submission.

CONSTRUCTION PERIOD

CP/J **Mobilisation**
Execution of building contract and hand over of site.
Application for statutory approvals.
Preparation of further Contractor's Proposals.

CP/K **Construction to Practical Completion**
Construction works up to and including practical completion.

CP/L **After Practical Completion**
Resolving defects and settling the final account.

Work Stage CP/A&B:

Appraisal and Strategic Briefing – Contractor's Proposals

CONTRACTOR CLIENT	ARCHITECT AS LEAD CONSULTANT	ARCHITECT AS DESIGNER AND DESIGN LEADER
Receive Employer's Requirements and Pre-tender H&S Plan Prepare and issue CC Policy Brief Identify any (employer) client's agent or another client Agree programme	Receive CC Policy Brief, incorporating Employer's Requirements and Pre-tender H&S Plan Review with contractor client the impact of CDM Regulations Agree programme	Receive CC Policy Brief, incorporating Employer's Requirements and Pre-tender H&S Plan Agree programme
Provide information about site/property condition and any operational hazards Obtain site information from employer if appropriate (CDM Reg 11)	Receive site information, visit site, appraise constraints[1] Identify site information required	Receive site information, visit site, appraise constraints[1] Identify site information required
Identify documents to accompany tender submission	Proceed to allocated Work Stage Identify documents to accompany tender submission	Proceed to allocated Work Stage Identify documents to accompany tender submission

Work Stage CP/C:

Outline Proposals – Contractor's Proposals

CONTRACTOR CLIENT	ARCHITECT AS LEAD CONSULTANT	ARCHITECT AS DESIGNER AND DESIGN LEADER
Authorise commencement of Work Stage	Commence Work Stage	Commence Work Stage
Consider evaluation and sustainable development, provide additional information required and instruct LC	Evaluate Employer's Requirements and CC Policy Brief[2] and consider findings with CC	Evaluate Employer's Requirements and CC Policy Brief[2] Advise on sustainable development
Consider request for surveys etc and instruct LC	Request approval for necessary site surveys, investigations etc and instruct CT	Identify surveys required *If instructed carry out or arrange and supervise agreed surveys*
Appoint additional consultants Consult PS as necessary	Identify requirement for additional consultants, request contractor client sanction	Establish design management procedures
Authorise Project Programme Advise on CC procedures Implement Work Stage procedures and programme	Prepare Project Programme Establish Work Stage procedures and programme	Advise on Project Programme Implement Work Stage and design management procedures and programme Prepare initial design studies
Consider design studies with design leader Sanction energy targets and fuel policy	 Request CC sanction to energy targets and fuel policy	Consider comment on design studies Consider design studies with client Advise on energy conservation, agree energy targets
	Review H&S risk assessments with PS	Initiate preliminary consultations with statutory authorities *(or other persons)* Review H&S risk assessments with PS
		Prepare Outline Proposals[3] and provide information for initial cost studies
Review Work Stage report and instruct LC	Prepare and submit Work Stage report and identify any instructions required	Contribute to Work Stage report, identify any instructions required
Advise decision about Outline Development Control submission	Review need for Outline Development Control approval, request instructions and direct CT	Consider need for Outline Development Control approval *If instructed make submission*
	Amend Outline Proposals if instructed to change (or comply with) the brief and direct CT	*Amend Outline Proposals if instructed to change (or comply with) the brief and direct CT*
	Request authority to proceed to next Work Stage	Obtain authority to proceed to next Work Stage via LC

Notes

[1] Assessment of physical, environmental, functional and regulatory constraints

[2] Consideration of time/cost/risks and environmental issues; identification of additional information required

[3] In accordance with the Employer's Requirements

QUANTITY SURVEYOR	STRUCTURAL ENGINEER	SERVICES ENGINEER	PLANNING SUPERVISOR
Receive CC Policy Brief, incorporating Employer's Requirements and Pre-tender H&S Plan	Receive CC Policy Brief, incorporating Employer's Requirements and Pre-tender H&S Plan	Receive CC Policy Brief, incorporating Employer's Requirements and Pre-tender H&S Plan	Receive CC Policy Brief incorporating Employer's Requirements and Pre-tender H&S Plan Review with contractor client the impact of CDM Regulations Notify project to HSE
Agree programme	Agree programme	Agree programme	
Receive site information, visit site, appraise constraints[1]	Receive site information, visit site, appraise constraints[1]	Receive site information, visit site, appraise constraints[1]	Receive site information, visit site, appraise constraints[1]
Identify site information required	Identify site information required	Identify site information required	Open H&S File for the project
Proceed to allocated Work Stage Identify documents to accompany tender submission	Proceed to allocated Work Stage Identify documents to accompany tender submission	Proceed to allocated Work Stage Identify documents to accompany tender submission	Proceed to allocated Work Stage
Commence Work Stage	Commence Work Stage	Commence Work Stage	Commence Work Stage
Evaluate Employer's Requirements and CC Policy Brief[2] Assess economic constraints	Evaluate Employer's Requirements and CC Policy Brief[2] Advise on sustainable development	Evaluate Employer's Requirements and CC Policy Brief[2] Advise on sustainable development	
	Identify surveys required *If instructed carry out or arrange and supervise agreed surveys*	Identify surveys required *If instructed carry out or arrange and supervise agreed surveys*	Advise on need for surveys in connection with H&S risks
			Advise contractor client about additional consultants, if requested
Advise on Project Programme Implement Work Stage and design management procedures and programme	Advise on Project Programme Implement Work Stage and design management procedures and programme	Advise on Project Programme Implement Work Stage and design management procedures and programme	Advise on Project Programme Implement Work Stage and design management procedures and programme
Advise on cost effect of design and energy options	Advise on structural aspects of design studies	Advise on services aspects of design studies, energy conservation, fuel policy, agree energy targets	Advise on safety aspects of design studies
Review H&S risk assessments with PS	Preliminary consultations with statutory authorities *(or others)* Review H&S risk assessments with PS	Preliminary consultations with statutory authorities *(or others)* Review H&S risk assessments with PS	Review H&S strategy and risk assessments with CT Develop H&S Plan
Prepare initial cost plan	Prepare Outline Proposals[3] and provide information for initial cost studies	Prepare Outline Proposals[3] and provide information for initial cost studies	
Contribute to Work Stage report, identify any instructions required	Contribute to Work Stage report, identify any instructions required	Contribute to Work Stage report, identify any instructions required	
	Provide information to support outline submission	*Provide information to support outline submission*	
Amend cost plan, including estimate and cash flow if instructed to change (or comply with) the brief	*Amend Outline Proposals if instructed to change (or comply with) the brief*	*Amend Outline Proposals if instructed to change (or comply with) the brief*	*Advise on H&S aspects of any proposed amendments to Outline Proposals*
Obtain authority to proceed to next Work Stage via LC	Obtain authority to proceed to next Work Stage via LC	Obtain authority to proceed to next Work Stage via LC	Obtain authority to proceed to next Work Stage via LC

Work Stage CP/D:

Detailed Proposals – Contractor's Proposals

CONTRACTOR CLIENT	ARCHITECT AS LEAD CONSULTANT	ARCHITECT AS DESIGNER AND DESIGN LEADER
Authorise commencement of Work Stage Implement Work Stage procedures and programme	Commence Work Stage Implement Work Stage procedures and programme	Commence Work Stage Implement Work Stage procedures and programme
	Evaluate Outline Proposals to establish compliance with CC Policy Brief	Evaluate Outline Proposals to establish compliance with CC Policy Brief
Sanction LC report as basis for detailed proposals and instruct any changes to CC Policy Brief	Co-ordinate results of CT studies, prepare interim report and request contractor client sanction to continue	Receive design/cost input from CT and develop detailed design solution
Consult PS as necessary, appoint additional consultants and specialist designers and advise LC	Identify requirement for additional consultants and/or specialists, request contractor client sanction	Identify requirement for additional consultants and/or specialists
Instruct LC on equipment tenders Provide details of fixed furniture and equipment to be provided in the building contract	Identify requirement for equipment selection tenders, request contractor client sanction	Prepare Detailed Proposals and outline specification Provide information for elemental cost plan
		Consult and negotiate as necessary to establish compliance in principle with statutory *(and other)* requirements
	Review design co-ordination with PS and CT	Review design co-ordination and development with PS; carry out risk assessments required Provide information to PS for H&S Plan and H&S File
Confirm CC Policy Brief now frozen		Consolidate Detailed Proposals[4]
Review Work Stage report, consider risks and any changes required and instruct LC	Prepare and submit Work Stage report and identify any instructions required	Contribute to Work Stage report, identify any instructions required
Authorise detailed Development Control submission	Request authority for Development Control submission and direct CT	Provide information to support detailed Development Control submission When instructed make submission
	Amend Detailed Proposals if instructed to change (or comply with) the brief and direct CT	*Amend Detailed Proposals if instructed to change (or comply with) the brief*
	Request authority to proceed to next Work Stage	Obtain authority to proceed to next Work Stage via LC

Notes
[4] To include means of escape, fire compartments, services space requirements, preliminary room layouts (if required)

QUANTITY SURVEYOR	STRUCTURAL ENGINEER	SERVICES ENGINEER	PLANNING SUPERVISOR
Commence Work Stage	Commence Work Stage	Commence Work Stage	Commence Work Stage
Implement Work Stage procedures and programme	Implement Work Stage procedures and programme	Implement Work Stage procedures and programme	Implement Work Stage procedures and programme
Evaluate Outline Proposals, complete any necessary cost studies to establish compliance with CC Policy Brief	Evaluate Outline Proposals, complete studies to establish compliance with CC Policy Brief	Evaluate Outline Proposals, complete studies to establish compliance with CC Policy Brief	Evaluate Outline Proposals to establish compliance with any H&S policy decisions in CC Policy Brief
Prepare elemental cost plan	Develop Outline Proposals to identify design constraints etc	Prepare schematic design (based on Outline Proposal)	
	Identify requirement for additional consultants and/or specialists	Identify requirement for additional consultants and/or specialists	*Advise contractor client about additional consultants or designers, if requested*
Continuously update cost plan, advise on critical elements	Prepare Detailed Proposals and outline specification Provide information for elemental cost plan	Prepare Detailed Proposals and outline specification Provide information for elemental cost plan	
Advise on cost effects of compliance with statutory *(and other)* requirements	Consider and consult as necessary to establish compliance in principle with statutory *(and other)* requirements	Consider and consult as necessary to establish compliance in principle with statutory *(and other)* requirements	
Review design co-ordination and development with PS; carry out risk assessments required Provide information to PS for H&S Plan and H&S File	Review design co-ordination and development with PS; carry out risk assessments required Provide information to PS for H&S Plan and H&S File	Review design co-ordination and development with PS; carry out risk assessments required Provide information to PS for H&S Plan and H&S File	Review design co-ordination and development with CT Identify additional risk assessments required Add relevant information to H&S Plan and H&S File
Prepare firm cost plan and cash flow projection	Update Detailed Proposals[4]	Update Detailed Proposals[4] Negotiate provision of incoming services	
Contribute to Work Stage report, identify any instructions required	Contribute to Work Stage report, identify any instructions required	Contribute to Work Stage report, identify any instructions required	Contribute to Work Stage report, identify any instructions required.
	Provide information to support detailed Development Control submission	Provide information to support detailed Development Control submission	
Amend cost plan, including estimate and cash flow if instructed to change (or comply with) the brief	*Amend Detailed Proposals if instructed to change (or comply with) the brief*	*Amend Detailed Proposals if instructed to change (or comply with) the brief*	*Advise on H&S aspects of any proposed amendments to Detailed Proposals*
Obtain authority to proceed to next Work Stage via LC	Obtain authority to proceed to next Work Stage via LC	Obtain authority to proceed to next Work Stage via LC	Obtain authority to proceed to next Work Stage via LC

Work Stage CP/E:

Final Proposals – Contractor's Proposals

CONTRACTOR CLIENT	ARCHITECT AS LEAD CONSULTANT	ARCHITECT AS DESIGNER AND DESIGN LEADER
Authorise commencement of Work Stage	Commence Work Stage	Commence Work Stage
Implement Work Stage procedures and programme	Implement Work Stage procedures and programme	Implement Work Stage procedures and programme
Sanction of final layouts	Request sanction for final layouts	Complete final layouts Receive and incorporate design information from CT Consult statutory authorities (and others) on developed design proposals, as necessary Agree positions for services terminals, ceiling layouts and major builders' work for services installations
	Make or request decisions necessary to maintain cost control	Provide information for continuous cost checks
		Complete Final Proposals
	Review design co-ordination and development, including design by specialist(s) with PS and CT	Review design co-ordination and development with PS; carry out risk assessments required Provide information to PS for H&S Plan
	Review design, cost plan and contingency plans	Review design, cost plan and contingency plans
Review Work Stage report, consider risks and any changes required and instruct LC	Prepare and submit Work Stage report and identify any instructions required	Contribute to Work Stage report, identify any instructions required
Authorise statutory and other submissions	Arrange programme and request contractor client sanction for preparation of submissions for statutory (and other) approvals	Provide information for and make (or support) submissions for statutory (and other) approvals
	Amend Final Proposals if instructed to change (or comply with) the brief and direct CT	*Amend Final Proposals if instructed to change (or comply with) the brief*
	Request authority to proceed to next Work Stage	Obtain authority to proceed to next Work Stage via LC

DESIGN (FINAL PROPOSALS) NOW FROZEN

Notes
NB: Stages CP/E and F are most likely to be implemented after stages G, H and acceptance of tender at stage J

QUANTITY SURVEYOR	STRUCTURAL ENGINEER	SERVICES ENGINEER	PLANNING SUPERVISOR
Commence Work Stage	Commence Work Stage	Commence Work Stage	Commence Work Stage
Implement Work Stage procedures and programme	Implement Work Stage procedures and programme	Implement Work Stage procedures and programme	Implement Work Stage procedures and programme
	Complete sizing of all structural elements Consult statutory authorities (and others) on developed design proposals, as necessary Provide for integration of services Provide for major builders' work for services installations	Complete final layouts and sizing Consult statutory authorities (and others) on developed design proposals, as necessary Arrange provision for services integration Agree positions for services terminals, ceiling layouts and major builders' work for services installations	
Continuously check cost of design against cost plan and advise LC	Provide information for cost checks	Provide information for cost checks	
	Complete Final Proposals	Complete Final Proposals	
Review design co-ordination and development with PS; carry out risk assessments required Provide information to PS for H&S Plan	Review design co-ordination and development with PS; carry out risk assessments required Provide information to PS for H&S Plan	Review design co-ordination and development with PS; carry out risk assessments required Provide information to PS for H&S Plan	Review design co-ordination policy with LC and CT Identify additional risk assessments required; update draft H&S Plan, add relevant information to H&S File
Prepare updated cost plan and cash flow projection Review design, cost plan and contingency plans	Review design, cost plan and contingency plans	Review design, cost plan and contingency plans	Review design, cost plan and contingency plans Review H&S strategy
Contribute to Work Stage report, identify any instructions required	Contribute to Work Stage report, identify any instructions required	Contribute to Work Stage report, identify any instructions required	Contribute to Work Stage report, identify any instructions required
Provide information to support statutory (and other) submissions	Provide information for and make (or support) submissions for statutory (and other) approvals	Provide information for and make (or support) submissions for statutory (and other) approvals	
Amend cost plan, including estimate and cash flow if instructed to change (or comply with) the brief	*Amend Final Proposals if instructed to change (or comply with) the brief*	*Amend Final Proposals if instructed to change (or comply with) the brief*	*Advise on H&S aspects of any proposed amendments to the Final Proposals*
Obtain authority to proceed to next Work Stage via LC	Obtain authority to proceed to next Work Stage via LC	Obtain authority to proceed to next Work Stage via LC	Obtain authority to proceed to next Work Stage via LC

Work Stage CP/F:

Production Information – Contractor's Proposals

CONTRACTOR CLIENT	ARCHITECT AS LEAD CONSULTANT	ARCHITECT AS DESIGNER AND DESIGN LEADER
Authorise commencement of Work Stage	Commence Work Stage	Commence Work Stage
Implement Work Stage procedures and programme	Implement Work Stage procedures and programme	Implement Work Stage procedures and programme
	F1: Review design co-ordination and development, including design by specialist(s), with PS and CT	F1: Prepare[5] co-ordinated production information to include: location drawings assembly drawings component drawings schedules : specification
	F2: Identify and agree programme for completion of outstanding production information[7]	F2: Identify and agree programme for completion of outstanding production information[7]
	Make or request decisions necessary to maintain cost control	Provide information for cost checks
Review Work Stage report, consider risks and any changes required and instruct LC	Prepare and submit Work Stage report and identify any instructions required from contractor client	Contribute to Work Stage report, identify any instructions required
	Amend production information if instructed to change (or comply with) the building contract and direct CT	*Amend production information if instructed to change (or comply with) the building contract*
	Request authority to proceed to next Work Stage	Obtain authority to proceed to next Work Stage via LC

Work Stage CP/G & H:

Tender Documentation and Tender Action – Contractor's Proposals

Assemble tender documents, including developed H&S Plan and submit to employer	Assist contractor client with assembly of tender submission documents	Provide tender submission documents
Respond to employer queries about tender submission	Assist CC to answer queries	Assist CC to answer queries
Carry out negotiations with employer	Assist CC with any negotiations with employer	Assist CC with any negotiations with employer

Notes

NB: Stages CP/E and F are most likely to be implemented after stages G, H and acceptance of tender (J)

[5] Includes receiving and integrating information from CT and specialists

[6] BSRIA definitions TN 8/94

ga = general arrangement

[7] Stage CP/F2 will only be required if production information (F1) required at tender stage H

Stages CP/J and possibly K will run in parallel with the completion of the design information

Note completion of statutory and other submissions is an activity under Stage J

QUANTITY SURVEYOR	STRUCTURAL ENGINEER	SERVICES ENGINEER	PLANNING SUPERVISOR
Commence Work Stage	Commence Work Stage	Commence Work Stage	Commence Work Stage
Implement Work Stage procedures and programme	Implement Work Stage procedures and programme	Implement Work Stage procedures and programme	Implement Work Stage procedures and programme
	F1: Prepare[5] co-ordinated production information to include: location drawings (ga) assembly drawings component drawings schedules : specification calculations	F1: Prepare [5] [6] co-ordinated production information to include: schematic drawings detailed design drawings co-ordination drawings builders work and fixings schedules: specification calculations	Review design co-ordination procedures with LC and CT Identify further information required for pre-tender H&S File
	F2: Identify and agree programme for completion of outstanding production information.[7]	F2: Identify and agree programme for completion of outstanding production information.[7]	
Continuously check cost of design against cost plan and advise LC	Provide information for cost checks	Provide information for cost checks	
Prepare updated cost plan Contribute to Work Stage report, identify any instructions required	Contribute to Work Stage report, identify any instructions required	Contribute to Work Stage report, identify any instructions required	Review H&S principles and time allocated for completion of project Contribute to Work Stage report, identify any instructions required
Amend cost plan if instructed to change (or comply with) the building contract	*Amend production information if instructed to change (or comply with) the building contract*	*Amend production information if instructed to change (or comply with) the building contract*	*Advise on H&S aspects of any proposed amendments*
Obtain authority to proceed to next Work Stage via LC	Obtain authority to proceed to next Work Stage via LC	Obtain authority to proceed to next Work Stage via LC	Obtain authority to proceed to next Work Stage via LC

QUANTITY SURVEYOR	STRUCTURAL ENGINEER	SERVICES ENGINEER	PLANNING SUPERVISOR
Provide tender submission documents	Provide tender submission documents	Provide tender submission documents	Assist with preparation of developed H&S Plan
Assist CC to answer queries	Assist CC to answer queries	Assist CC to answer queries	Assist employer or CC to answer queries in relation to H&S Plan
Assist CC with any negotiations with employer	Assist CC with any negotiations with employer	Assist CC with any negotiations with employer	Assist CC with any negotiations with employer

Work Stage CP/J:

Mobilisation – Contractor's Proposals

EMPLOYER AND/OR EMPLOYER'S AGENT	CONTRACTOR CLIENT	ARCHITECT AS LEAD CONSULTANT	ARCHITECT AS DESIGNER AND DESIGN LEADER
Consider acceptance of tender and appointment of principal contractor (CDM Regs) Ascertain H&S Plan sufficiently developed for construction phase to commence	Receive notification of acceptance of tender and appointment of principal contractor (CDM Regs) and that H&S Plan is sufficiently developed		
Agree administrative arrangements with CC	Authorise commencement of Work Stage. Implement Work Stage procedures and programme	Commence Work Stage Implement Work Stage procedures and programme	Commence Work Stage Implement Work Stage and design management procedures and programme
	Agree administrative arrangements with CT and EA	Agree administrative arrangements with CC	Implement administrative arrangements
Despatch contract documents to contractor for checking and execution. On return, execution by employer (client) Despatch certified true copy of contract documents to CC	Provide documents required for the building contract Receive, check and execute contract; return to EA	Collate documents required for the building contract	Provide copies of documents required for the building contract Issue production information as required
	Instruct completion of outstanding production information required [7] (further Contractor's Proposals)	Request authority to implement programme for completion of outstanding production information[7] and direct CT	
		Co-ordinate completion of all statutory (and other) submissions	Complete all statutory (and other) submissions
Review further Contractor's Proposals and send comments to CC	Despatch further Contractor's Proposals Consider EA's comments and instruct LC	Collate further Contractor's Proposals *Amend Contractor's Proposals if instructed to change (or comply with) the building contract and direct CT*	Prepare and issue further Contractor's Proposals *Amend Contractor's Proposals if instructed to change (or comply with) the building contract*

Notes

[7] Stage CP/F2 will only be required if production information (F1) required at tender stage H

QUANTITY SURVEYOR	STRUCTURAL ENGINEER	SERVICES ENGINEER	PLANNING SUPERVISOR
Commence Work Stage Implement Work Stage and design management procedures and programme Implement administrative arrangements	Commence Work Stage Implement Work Stage and design management procedures and programme Implement administrative arrangements	Commence Work Stage Implement Work Stage and design management procedures and programme Implement administrative arrangements	Commence Work Stage Implement Work Stage and design management procedures and programme Implement administrative arrangements
Contribute to assembly of contract documents	Contribute to assembly of contract documents	Contribute to assembly of contract documents	Review design co-ordination procedures in respect of further Contractor's Proposals and co-ordinate with employer's compliance review Notify further particulars to HSE
	Complete all statutory (*and other*) submissions	Complete all statutory (*and other*) submissions	
Check cost of further Contractor's Proposals *Amend cost plan if instructed to change (or comply with) the building contract*	Prepare and issue further Contractor's Proposals *Amend Contractor's Proposals if instructed to change (or comply with) the building contract*	Prepare and issue further Contractor's Proposals *Amend Contractor's Proposals if instructed to change (or comply with) the building contract*	*Advise on proposed amendments to production information*

Work Stage CP/K:

Construction to Practical Completion – Contractor's Proposals

EMPLOYER AND OR EMPLOYER'S AGENT	CONTRACTOR CLIENT	ARCHITECT AS LEAD CONSULTANT	ARCHITECT AS DESIGNER AND DESIGN LEADER
Arrange hand-over of site	Take possession of site Perform the obligations of the contractor under the building contract		
Review further Contractor's Proposals and send comments to CC	Despatch further Contractor's Proposals Consider EA's comments and instruct LC	Collate further Contractor's Proposals *If instructed arrange for amendment of Contractor's Proposals to change (or comply with) the building contract and direct CT*	Prepare and issue further Contractor's Proposals *If instructed arrange for amendment of Contractor's Proposals to change (or comply with) the building contract*
Consider proposed change instructions Arrange co-ordination of H&S File with information to be provided by employer's consultants (if any) and CC	Receive change instructions Provide quotation and obtain PS sanction where appropriate Continuously assemble data for H&S File[8]	*Collate information for change instructions; obtain PS sanction assist in preparation of CC's quotation where appropriate* Collate information from CT for H&S File[8]	Advise on the need for change instructions *If instructed provide information for change instructions* Assist with co-ordination of H&S File[8]
Honour certificate by due date Ascertain loss and/or expense if required	Calculate and apply for interim payments		
Receive regular progress reports Attend or conduct progress and performance review meetings	Consider progress and financial statements and instruct CT Hold progress and review meetings as necessary	Collate and submit CT reports to CC Attend CC's or EA's meetings as appropriate	Make site visits (as Agreement) and report to LC Attend CC's or EA's meetings as appropriate
Agree procedures for and carrying out commissioning and testing of services	Agree commissioning and testing procedures with EC/EA	Co-ordinate commissioning and testing procedures for services, including drainage, with CC	
Attend meeting and receive Works for occupation or use Receive keys from CC and H&S File from PS	Confirm all works are complete Attend hand over meeting Agree defects reporting procedure	Attend hand-over meeting Agree defects reporting procedure	Attend hand-over meeting
Implement defects reporting procedure	Submit application for interim payment	Issue updated status report	

Work Stage CP/L:

After Practical Completion – Contractor's Proposals

EMPLOYER AND OR EMPLOYER'S AGENT	CONTRACTOR CLIENT	ARCHITECT AS LEAD CONSULTANT	ARCHITECT AS DESIGNER AND DESIGN LEADER
Report defects that require immediate attention as they occur	Receive defect reports Correct defects in accordance with agreed procedure	Receive defect reports, determine necessary action and advise CC	Advise on necessary action to remedy defects
Honour interim certificates	Assemble data and agree matters for final account / Final Statement Calculate and apply for interim payments as necessary		
Co-ordinate pre-final inspections, collate and issue of schedules of defects, including incomplete work Agree programme for execution of any remedial works with CC Appoint PS if necessary	Collaborate in pre-final inspections Agree programme for execution of remedial works with employer/EA Advise client if planning supervisor should be (re)appointed to prepare H&S Plan for repair of any major defects	Collaborate in pre-final inspections	Collaborate in pre-final inspections
When contractor confirms work is complete, arrange and make final inspection Issue statement of making good defects	Confirm that all remedial works are complete Receive statement(s) of making good defects		
Agree final account Issue and honour final statement	Complete final account and agree with employer Make application for final payment	Advise CC that (consultant) Services are complete	Advise CC that (consultant) Services are complete

QUANTITY SURVEYOR	STRUCTURAL ENGINEER	SERVICES ENGINEER	PLANNING SUPERVISOR
	Prepare and issue further Contractor's Proposals *If instructed arrange for amendment of Contractor's Proposals to change (or comply with) the building contract*	Prepare and issue further Contractor's Proposals *If instructed arrange for amendment of Contractor's Proposals to change (or comply with) the building contract*	*Review further Contractor's Proposals, ensure H&S implications have been considered*
Estimate cost of proposed or issued change instructions	Advise on the need for change instructions If instructed provide information for change instructions Assist with co-ordination of H&S File[8]	Advise on the need for change instructions *If instructed provide information for change instructions* Assist with co-ordination of H&S File[8]	*Examine draft design change instructions to contractor, ensure H&S implications have been considered and relevant information provided to CC*
Assist with calculation of interim payments due. If instructed, assist with evaluation of claims			
Prepare regular cost reports including out-turn cost and cash flow Attend CC's or EA's meetings as appropriate	Make site visits (as Agreement) and report to LC Attend CC's or EA's meetings as appropriate	Make site visits (as Agreement) and report to LC Attend CC's or EA's meetings as appropriate	Receive, review and collate information from employer's consultants CC and CT and add to H&S File
Review and issue updated cost report at completion	Attend hand-over meeting	Attend hand-over meeting	Deliver completed H&S File to employer. Advise on secure storage and future use of File
Calculate interim payment			Advise client that (consultant) Services are complete

QUANTITY SURVEYOR	STRUCTURAL ENGINEER	SERVICES ENGINEER	PLANNING SUPERVISOR
	Advise on necessary action to remedy defects	Advise on necessary action to remedy defects	**Notes** [8] The contractor may also be required to provide: 'drawings and information showing or describing the Works as built, and concerning the maintenance operation of the Works, including any installations comprised in the Works, as may be specified…' (clause 5.5 JCT WCD 98) and; acceptance test results, commissioning records, certificates for building services installations
Obtain information required to settle final account within time stated in contract *If instructed, assist with evaluation of claims*			
Assist with calculation of interim payments as necessary Update last cost report if predicted out-turn cost changes	Collaborate in pre-final inspections	Collaborate in pre-final inspections	
Complete final account and agree with contractor client (and employer) Advise client that (consultant) Services are complete	Advise client that (consultant) Services are complete	Advise client that (consultant) Services are complete	

References

GLOSSARY

Definitions of some of the terms used in this document, and where appropriate indicating the source of the definition. Also includes cross-references to variants of the terms used.

Personnel

Architect: a consultant, usually the lead consultant, design leader, designer and contract administrator/employer's agent.

Client: appoints the consultant team; the term used in CDM Regulations; also called 'Employer' in building contracts.

Client's representative: appointed to act with authority by the client, also called 'Project Sponsor' by Government departments or 'Project Director' by NHS. May be a consultant project manager. *See also employer's agent.*

Consultant: a person or firm appointed by the client to perform professional services.

Consultant team: group of consultants preparing designs and production information (or Employer's Requirements for design and build contracts), normally with duties during construction to inspect Works for compliance; also called 'Design Team' and in *JCT Management Contract 1998* 'Professional Team'.

Contract administrator: used as optional alternative title to 'Architect' in most JCT building contracts; required to issue certificates, instructions etc.

Contractor: a contractor appointed by the client to execute or procure the execution of all or part of the project or the Works and to co-ordinate and supervise or procure the co-ordination and supervision of such execution *(ACE)*. Under a design and build building contract a contractor is responsible for the completion of the design and construction of the project.

(Designers) the term used in CDM Regulations for any person or firm providing design services.

Design leader: usually the architect, with responsibility for directing and co-ordinating the design process *(RIBA SFA/99)*.

(Design team) *See 'Consultant team'.*

(Design team leader) *See 'Lead consultant' and 'Design leader'.*

Employer: the term used in the building contract for the client.

Employer's agent: acts for the employer/client; does not certify under *JCT 'With Contractor's Design' 1998*.

Employer/client: the term used in connection with design and build procurement. Responsible for performance of the employer/client's obligations under the Agreement.

Lead consultant: responsible for co-ordination and integration of other consultants activities; usually the 'Architect' *(duties defined in RIBA SFA/99)*.

Planning supervisor: the person appointed to fulfil statutory duties under the CDM Regulations, responsible *(as RIBA form PS/99)* for preparing pre-tender Health and Safety Plan and Health and Safety File.

(Professional team) *See 'Consultant team'.*

Quantity surveyor: the consultant responsible for cost advice, valuation of Works executed etc with duties under JCT building contracts (NB a 'designer' under CDM Regs).

Services engineer: the consultant responsible for mechanical and electrical services.

Specialist (or Specialist Designer): in this context, usually a contractor providing design services for an element of the scheme.

Structural engineer: the consultant responsible for structural matters.

Sub-contractor: a person or firm appointed by or on behalf of a contractor to execute part of the project or of the Works or to manufacture or supply material for incorporation therein *(ACE)*.

Documentation

Brief: 'At inception, the initial statement of requirements. At the commencement of design (Work Stage C) the client's requirements developed after consideration of any feasibility studies and set out in the Strategic Brief. After approval of the Detailed Proposals (Work Stage D) the detailed written Project Brief developed in conjunction with the client and that design, unless and until varied by the client.' *(RIBA SFA/99, etc.)*

Builder's work drawings:

at Design Stage: 'to show provision required to accommodate services which significantly affect the building structure fabric and external works. Also drawings and schedules of work to be carried out by building trades';

at Installation Stage: 'to show requirements for building works necessary to facilitate the installation of engineering services (other than where it is appropriate to mark out on site)'. *(BSRIA)*

Contractor's Proposals: The Contractor's Proposals for completing the design of the project under a design and build building contract.

Co-ordinated production information: A set of

References

conventions for preparation of the information to be issued for construction, comprising *(CPIC)*:

Location drawings: 'Drawings up to 1:50 scale showing layouts and relationships and a key to more detailed information on 'Assembly drawings'; also called 'General arrangement drawings' see also 'Sketch drawings (M&E).'

Assembly drawings: detail drawings, usually at 1:20 or 1:10 or larger scales, showing how different elements relate, may also give specification references.

Component drawings: drawings giving information necessary for the manufacture of particular components.

Specifications

Bills of quantities

Co-ordination drawings: Drawings showing the interrelationship of two or more engineering drawings services and their relation to the structure and building fabric, at least 1:50 scale with some sections at 1:20. *(BSRIA)*

Cost plan: A document showing the estimated cost of all parts of the project and how it is to be spent. *(ACE)*

Employer's Requirements: The specified requirements of the client to be incorporated into a Design and Build contract.

Installation drawings: Drawings based on Detailed design or Co-ordination drawings, 'with the primary purpose of defining information needed by the workforce on site to install the works'. *(BSRIA)*

Shop drawings: Drawings produced for the purpose of explaining how the components of the designs are to be fabricated. *(ACE)*

BIBLIOGRAPHY

The Architect's contract. A Guide to RIBA Forms of Appointment 1999 and other Architect's appointments
RIBA Publications Ltd, ISBN 1 85946 054 2, 1999

Architect's Job Book Sixth Edition (Seventh Edition due Autumn 2000)
RIBA Publications Ltd, ISBN 1 85946 007 0, 1995

Design management systems BS 7000 Part 4
British Standards Institution, 1996

Briefing the Team (Construction Industry Board)
Thomas Telford Publishing, ISBN 0 7277 2541 6, 1997

Generic Design and Construction Process Protocol
University of Salford, ISBN 0 902896 17 2, 1998

Co-ordinated Project information
Co-ordinating Committee for Project Information (now construction Production Information Committee), ISBN 0 9512662 3 3, 1987

The allocation of design responsibilities for building engineering services
BSRIA Technical note TN 8/94, ISBN 0 86022 371X, 1994

Various Forms of Appointment/Conditions of Engagement
Published by RIBA, ACE and RICS